DIRECTOR MANUAL

Group

Loveland, Colorado

www.group.com/vbs

Incredible things will happen™

Avalanche Ranch Director Manual

Visit our Web sites:
www.group.com
www.group.com/vbs
www.groupoutlet.com

Unless otherwise indicated, all Scripture quotations are taken from the *Holy Bible*, New Living Translation, copyright © 1996, 2004. Used by permission of Tyndale House Publishers, Inc., Wheaton, Illinois 60189. All rights reserved.

A special thanks to our team of top-notch field test **Ranch Crew Leaders:** Tatiana Bido, Lois Debner, Candy DeVore, Spring Heflin, Dana Jamgochian, Sarah Little, Cindy Ward, Dan Ward, and Katie Williams.

Thanks to our talented VBS curriculum team:
Jody Brolsma, Stephen Caine, Shelly Dillon, Lyndsay Gerwing, Cindy S. Hansen, Elisa Hansen, Lisa Harris, Deb Helmers, Tracy K. Hindman, Kate Holburn, Julia Martin, Kari K. Monson, Barbie Murphy, Peggy Naylor, Joani Schultz, and Rodney Stewart.

ISBN 978-0-7644-3249-1
Printed in the United States of America.
10 9 8 7 6 5 4 3 2 1   09 08 07

DIRECTOR MANUAL

CONTENTS

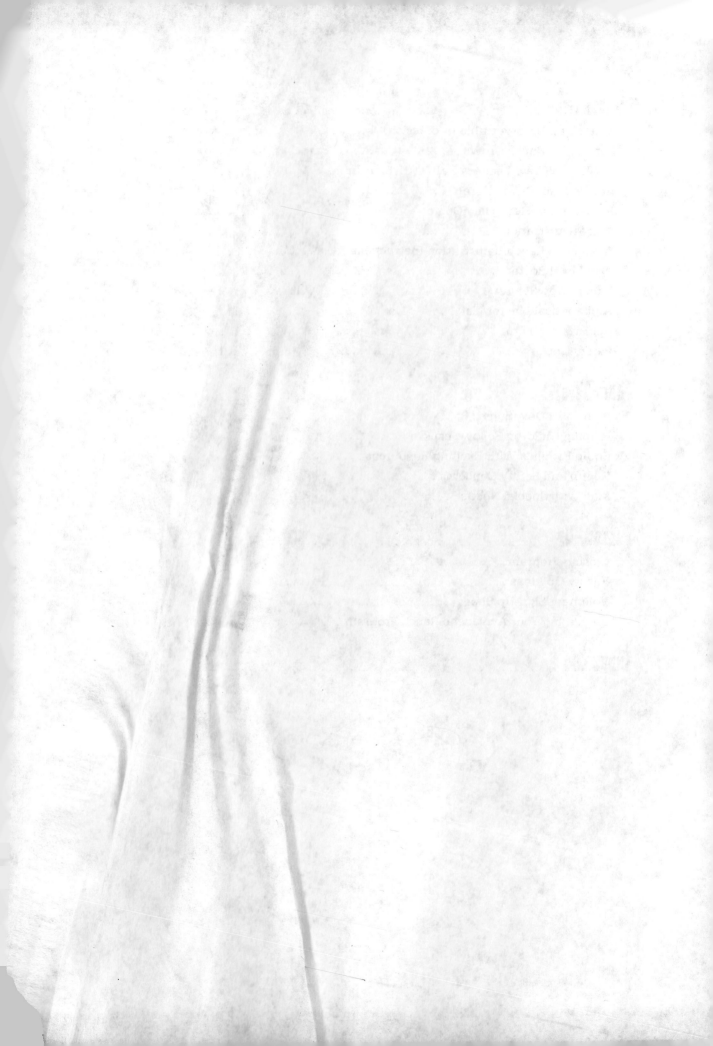

Welcome to Avalanche Ranch!

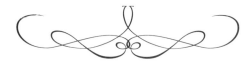

Get ready for a wild ride through God's Word...at Avalanche Ranch!

WAH-HOO!

Welcome to Avalanche Ranch, a wild ride through God's Word! Get ready for an exciting celebration of God's love filled with amazing Bible adventures, unforgettable songs, memory-making crafts, and life-changing missions.

Avalanche Ranch is overflowing with fun for kids, teenagers, and adults. Everyone involved in *this* VBS will jump into God's Word... and will never be the same again! As kids explore amazing Bible adventures, they will take part in Daily Challenges that encourage them to apply Bible truths to everyday life.

If you haven't used Group's VBS materials before, you're in for a fun time. Avalanche Ranch is an exciting, fun-filled, Bible-based program your kids will love. (We know because we tested everything in a field test last summer. Look for the "Field Test Findings" to learn how our discoveries will make *your* program the best!)

Kids start each day by forming small groups called Ranch Crews. All the Ranch Crews gather at Sing & Play Stampede to sing and do fun motions to upbeat Bible songs that introduce kids to the concepts they will be learning that day. Then Ranch Crews visit five different Ranch Stations.

They sample tasty treats at Chuck Wagon Chow, go on Wild Bible Adventures, make delightful creations in Cowpoke Crafts and Missions, have fun at Horseplay Games, and meet Chadder Chipmunk™ on video! Each day, one group will even star in a fun PowerPoint presentation, called Spotlight Drama. Then everyone comes together for the closing, Showtime Roundup. And throughout the week, children work on a special project they will share during Operation Kid-to-Kid™. This missions project allows the participants of all ages at your church to impact needy children in Africa!

This Director Manual contains everything you need to plan a successful program, recruit and train volunteers, publicize your program, and follow up with participants after Avalanche Ranch comes to an end.

Trail Tip

As the Avalanche Ranch Director, you want to know what's happening each day. Refer to the Avalanche Ranch Overview chart on pages 10-11 to get an overview of the Bible stories and biblical truths elementary kids cover. You'll discover how these truths are reinforced creatively throughout each day.

Field Test Findings

Afraid you'll feel lost once you distribute those station leader manuals? Don't worry! The chart on the following pages contains all the information you'll need to have an idea of what's happening in each station. Veteran VBS directors tell us that it's nice to simply delegate and give some of the responsibility to the station leaders.

Now let's start a stampede to *your* Avalanche Ranch!

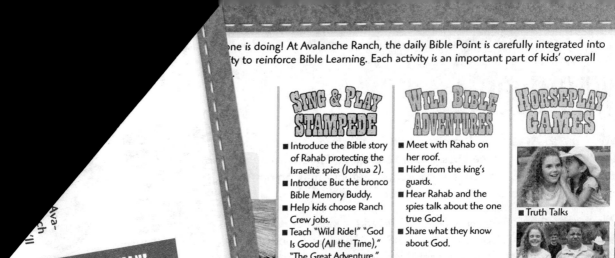

...one is doing! At Avalanche Ranch, the daily Bible Point is carefully integrated into ...ty to reinforce Bible Learning. Each activity is an important part of kids' overall

SING & PLAY STAMPEDE

WILD BIBLE ADVENTURES

HORSEPLAY GAMES

INTRODUCTION

...God is real.

Bible Story: Rahab protects the Israelite spies (Joshua 2).

SING & PLAY STAMPEDE
- Introduce the Bible story of Rahab protecting the Israelite spies (Joshua 2).
- Introduce Buc the bronco Bible Memory Buddy.
- Help kids choose Ranch Crew jobs.
- Teach "Wild Ride!" "God Is Good (All the Time)," "The Great Adventure," and "This Is the Day" (Psalm 118:24).

WILD BIBLE ADVENTURES
- Meet with Rahab on her roof.
- Hide from the king's guards.
- Hear Rahab and the spies talk about the one true God.
- Share what they know about God.

HORSEPLAY GAMES
- Truth Talks
- Spy Sneak
- One a...

DAY 2

Treasure Verse: "For the Lord your God is with you wherever you go" (Joshua 1:9).

Bible Point: God is with us.

Bible Story: The Israelites cross the Jordan River (Joshua 3-4).

SING & PLAY STAMPEDE
- Introduce the Bible story about the Israelites crossing the Jordan River (Joshua 3-4).
- Introduce Shadow the cattle dog Bible Memory Buddy.
- Teach "Forever," "Worship You Forever," and "Praise the Lord" (Psalm 150:6).

WILD BIBLE ADVENTURES
- Take off their shoes and walk on wet ground near the Jordan River.
- Act out the Israelites crossing the Jordan River.
- Watch the "river" miraculously stop flowing.
- Create stone memorials of God's presence.

HORSEPLAY GAMES

- Calf and Cattle Dog

- Jordan Memorial
- Shadow...

DAY 3

Treasure Verse: "The Lord is my strength" (Psalm 118:14).

Bible Point: God is strong.

Bible Story: The walls of Jericho crash down (Joshua 6).

SING & PLAY STAMPEDE
- Introduce the Bible story about the walls of Jericho crashing down (Joshua 6).
- Introduce Ranger the bison Bible Memory Buddy.
- Teach "You Are My All in All" and "Awesome God."

WILD BIBLE ADVENTURES
- Join a sergeant in Joshua's army and take part in a military drill.
- Become the walls of Jericho.
- Write on a paper brick hard things they're going through.

HORSEPLAY GAMES
- No Smiling!

- Empty the Pail
- Safe in t...

DAY 4

Treasure Verse: "For the Lord Most High is awesome" (Psalm 47:2).

Bible Point: God is awesome.

Bible Story: Jesus dies and rises again (Mark 15-16).

SING & PLAY STAMPEDE
- Introduce the Bible story about how Jesus dies and rises again (Mark 15-16).
- Introduce Skye the eagle Bible Memory Buddy.
- Teach "Were You There."

WILD BIBLE ADVENTURES
- Wear a black armband to mourn Jesus' death.
- Hide and listen to two women who discover that Jesus is alive.
- Celebrate Jesus' resurrection.
- Receive a glow bracelet as a reminder to share the good news of Jesus' love.

HORSEPLAY GAMES

- Watering-Hole Relay

- Ice Tag
- This Is a...

DAY 5

Treasure Verse: "If you love me, obey my commandments" (John 14:15).

Bible Point: God is in charge.

Bible Story: God heals Naaman (2 Kings 5).

SING & PLAY STAMPEDE
- Introduce the Bible story about God healing Naaman (2 Kings 5).
- Introduce Boss the longhorn bull Bible Memory Buddy.
- Review Sing & Play Stampede songs.

WILD BIBLE ADVENTURES
- Hear about a disease called leprosy.
- Have smelly onion rubbed on their hands.
- Discover an amazing way to get rid of "onionitis."
- Explore what it means that God is in charge.

HORSEPLAY GAMES

- Seven Showers
- Follow th...

- Who's the Boss?

Refer to the chart to see how each station's activities supplement other activities and help kids get wild about God's Word.

CHUCK WAGON CHOW	CHADDER'S WILD WEST THEATER	COWPOKE CRAFTS & MISSIONS	SHOWTIME ROUNDUP
  Spy Guy Trail Mix	 Will Chadder *ever* become a real cowboy?	 Buddy Bags	■ Review the Treasure Verse (Jeremiah 10:10) from the Bible. ■ Demonstrate "real" by using an extension cord, fan, and light. ■ Sing songs to celebrate our real God. ■ Take home Daily Challenge® reminders to show others that God is real.
 Stick With Us S'mores	 Will Snake succeed in stealing the herd?	  Prayer Journals  Shining Star Memorials	■ Review the Treasure Verse (Joshua 1:9). ■ Act out Joshua and the Israelites crossing the Jordan River. ■ Pray, sing, and celebrate that God is with us. ■ Take home Daily Challenge reminders to show others that God is with us.
 Tumbling Jericho Walls	 How will Chadder and Calamity Jean survive?	 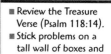 Operation Kid-to-Kid™ Prayer Bears	■ Review the Treasure Verse (Psalm 118:14). ■ Stick problems on a tall wall of boxes and watch them tumble down. ■ Sing songs, thanking God for his strength. ■ Take home Daily Challenge reminders to show others that God is strong.
 esome Avalanche Surprise	 Did Buck fall over the cliff?	Boot Birdhouses  Wild West Chalkboards	■ Thank Jesus for his awesome gift of eternal life. ■ Review the Treasure Verse (Psalm 47:2). ■ Sing worshipful songs as they thank Jesus for being our Savior. ■ Take home Daily Challenge reminders to show others that God is awesome.
 Naaman's Dip	 What crazy concoction will chef Chadder cook up?	Make-Your-Own Sheriff's Badge Cattle Drive Maze	■ Remember what they've learned at Avalanche Ranch. ■ Review the Treasure Verse (John 14:15). ■ Present their Operation Kid-to-Kid™ Prayer Bears as an offering to God. ■ Take home Daily Challenge reminders to show others that God is in charge.

Avalanche Ranch Basics

We've rounded up answers to all your questions right here!

AVALANCHE RANCH IS DIFFERENT!

It may seem that all VBS programs are alike. But take a closer look, and you'll see why Group's VBS is the most effective VBS around!

At Avalanche Ranch, kids learn one important Bible Point each day. Instead of trying to teach kids more than they can remember or apply, Avalanche Ranch focuses on one key biblical concept. The Bible Point is reinforced daily through Bible stories, Bible verses, songs, and hands-on activities that help kids know more about God. Kids who attend your church regularly will enjoy discovering this important truth in fresh, new ways. And neighborhood kids who come to your VBS will hear the "meat" of the gospel right away. Each day kids will learn something new about God:

Day 1: God is real.

Day 2: God is with us.

Day 3: God is strong.

Day 4: God is awesome.

Day 5: God is in charge.

At Avalanche Ranch, kids live what they've learned every day! Through the Daily Challenge, kids live out each Bible Point at home! You've never seen life application like this before. See page 17 for more information about the Daily Challenge.

At Avalanche Ranch, kids learn the way they learn best. Not all kids learn the same way, so Avalanche Ranch offers seven daily Ranch Stations to meet the needs of all kinds of learners. Children will come away from each day remembering the Bible Point because each child will pick it up in a way that matches his or her learning style.

Sing & Play Stampede's songs and motions will teach the Bible Point to your **musical learners**. Plus, it's where kids worship God with gusto!

Horseplay Games, Wild Bible Adventures, and Cowpoke Crafts and Missions allow **bodily-kinesthetic learners** to wiggle and move as they explore the Bible Point in active ways. Through Operation Kid-to-Kid, you'll help the kids at your VBS develop hearts for needy children.

Chadder's Wild West Theater lets **visual learners** discover the Bible Point through watching the high-adventure cliffhanger *Chadder's Wild West*

Field Test Findings

Don't overlook the impact this program can have on teenagers and adults. Learners of all ages benefit from the active, fresh Bible story presentations at Avalanche Ranch. We've heard from youth and adults who said their hearts were touched, lives were changed, and faith was renewed after experiencing these Bible truths in such new ways! Plus, now Group offers a program designed specifically for youth!

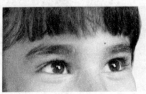

Adventure. Kids also have a chance to read, think, and explore colorful, eye-catching Wild Ride Bible Guides! Plus, they will receive engaging Bible Memory Buddies® to help remind them of the day's Treasure Verse!

Chuck Wagon Chow allows **interpersonal learners** the opportunity to explore Jesus' love as they make and serve snacks for all the participants at Avalanche Ranch.

Showtime Roundup's dramatic and interactive programs help **linguistic learners** remember each day's Bible Point and Treasure Verse.

Leaders at every Ranch Station ask meaningful, thought-provoking questions that encourage **logical and introspective learners** to think about and apply the Bible Point. We've even added questions to the Crew Leader Pocket Guides so your crew leaders will be prepared for life-changing discussions.

At Avalanche Ranch, teachers teach the way they teach best. Just like kids, not all teachers think alike. Instead of forcing every teacher to teach the same material, Avalanche Ranch provides opportunities for you to place a variety of teachers in the roles that best suit them. Have a great storyteller in your congregation? Recruit that person to lead Wild Bible Adventures. Have a great athlete? Recruit that person to lead Horseplay Games. Because each Ranch Station is different, teachers can volunteer in their areas of expertise. And volunteers who are intimidated by the idea of teaching can join your staff as Ranch Crew Leaders.

At Avalanche Ranch, no activity stands alone. Instead of leading independent, isolated classes, station leaders see all the kids each day. Sing & Play Stampede songs play in the background during other activities. Activities from Wild Bible Adventures are used at Showtime Roundup. Kids create Operation Kid-to-Kid Prayer Bears during Cowpoke Crafts and Missions and then donate them as an offering during Showtime Roundup. Bible Memory Buddies appear in Sing & Play Stampede and Chadder's Wild West Theater. The Horseplay Games Leader serves as an assistant Spotlight Drama Leader. Each member of your team provides a unique and important part of kids' total VBS experience. With everyone working together, your staff will breeze through the week.

Field Test Findings
We've heard it again and again from VBS directors everywhere: "This program brought out people's talents in wonderful new ways! People who never imagined that they could work with kids had a great time—and already volunteered to help next year!" So go for it! Look beyond "the usual" group of volunteers, and bring in some new faces.

> **Awesome leaders are the secret to a great Avalanche Ranch adventure!**

Because each activity plays an important role, it's essential that each station leader follow the activities in his or her leader manual. We've visited VBS programs where one leader wanted to change a song or activity, only to discover that it was an important building block for learning in another station. Remind your staff to do the program as it's written so kids can get the most out of every activity.

Field Test Findings

Churches around the country have reported great success with having families travel together as crews. Family crews build unity, encourage communication, and create wonderful memories that families will cherish for years to come. It really works!

At Avalanche Ranch, kids have important roles. Throughout the week, kids travel to stations with their Ranch Crews—small groups of three to five kids. On the first day, each child chooses a job that he or she will do throughout the week. Kids may be Readers, Ranch Guides, Materials Managers, Coaches, or Prayer People. From time to time, station leaders will call on kids to complete tasks that are part of their job descriptions.

Each Ranch Crew also has an adult or teenage Ranch Crew Leader. Ranch Crew Leaders aren't teachers. They're simply part of Ranch Crew families—like older brothers or sisters. Ranch Crew Leaders participate in all the activities and encourage kids to talk about and apply what they're learning. Ranch Crew Leaders who participated in Avalanche Ranch field tests saw kids encouraging other kids during the activities, helping younger crew members with difficult tasks, and reminding each other to use kind words. Kids put God's love into action!

At Avalanche Ranch, everyone is treated with respect. Because elementary kids travel in combined-age Ranch Crews, big kids and little kids learn to work together. Instead of trying to compete with children their own age, older children help younger children during Cowpoke Crafts and Missions and Horseplay Games. Younger children spark older children's imaginations during Wild Bible Adventures and Showtime Roundup.

Think of Ranch Crews as families in which kids naturally learn with and from one another. Social skills improve, self-esteem rises, cooperation increases, and discipline problems diminish.

Combined-age Ranch Crews also allow people of any age (even entire families) to join you at Avalanche Ranch. You can even use combined-age crews to teach kids about being part of the body of Christ!

Knowing and understanding these distinctions will help you present Avalanche Ranch to your church or committee.

THE DAILY CHALLENGE®

Of course you want kids to come to Avalanche Ranch and learn about God. But imagine how life-changing it would be if kids took what they learned, applied it *right away* to daily life, and showed God's love in real life.

That's where the Daily Challenge comes in! It's as easy as one, two, three!

1. Build your corral. Work with your Sing & Play Stampede Leader to build a simple corral fence from cinder blocks and cardboard tubes. The corral will decorate the front of your Sing & Play Stampede area. For the ultimate in ease, follow the steps on page 18.

2. Let kids choose their challenge! While kids eat their Chuck Wagon Chow snacks, they will look over that day's Daily Challenges, found in the back of each Wild Ride Bible Guide. Crew members will work together to choose which challenge they will do before they come back to Avalanche Ranch. Kids will place Wow Cow stickers (included in their Wild Ride Bible Guides) next to their chosen challenges.

At the end of the day, the Showtime Roundup Leader will have elementary kids take that day's Daily Challenge from their Bible Guides. Kids will look at the Daily Challenge again to help them remember what challenges they chose. Then each child will use an Avalanche Ranch sticker to hold the Daily Challenge around his or her wrist. Each day, kids will wear a new Daily Challenge home!

3. Watch the stampede! On Day 2, the Sing & Play Stampede Leader will ask kids to gather with their crews and talk about how they carried out their Daily Challenge. At a designated time, crew leaders will take a Daily Challenge Wow Cow and tape it to the fence so the silly cows look like they're looking over the fence. As the Wow Cows join your Ranch, VBS participants will sing "The Great Adventure."

You'll round up easy ways for kids to share God's love!

Trail Tip

Daily Challenge Wow Cows are available from Group Publishing or your local Group supplier.

Field Test Findings

Remember that your goal is to encourage kids to practice what they're learning *just for the joy of serving Jesus!* Don't offer bribes, incentives, or crew competitions to entice kids to complete their Daily Challenges. We discovered that kids didn't need any other motivation; they were excited about choosing a challenge and living it out! Focus on intrinsic motivation (from the heart), not extrinsic motivation (for external factors).

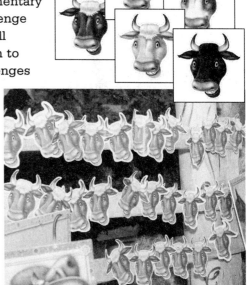

BUILDING YOUR DAILY CHALLENGE® CORRAL

In order to show kids that they're spreading God's Word through the Daily Challenges, you'll need to prepare the Daily Challenge Corral in the Sing & Play Stampede area. Here's how we made ours. These instructions are so easy that you almost don't need pictures!

FIRST, gather cardboard tubes (from fabric stores or carpet stores), cinder blocks, brown paint, and paintbrushes (from building supply stores).

Trail Tip Build the Daily Challenge® Corral high enough so kids can watch the herd of Wow Cows grow. You may want to stack the cinder blocks on wooden crates.

Trail Tip Keep kids away from the cinder blocks so the cinder blocks don't tip over. Set the cinder blocks on the stage where kids won't be playing, or set them behind bales of hay or other props.

NEXT, paint the cardboard tubes brown.

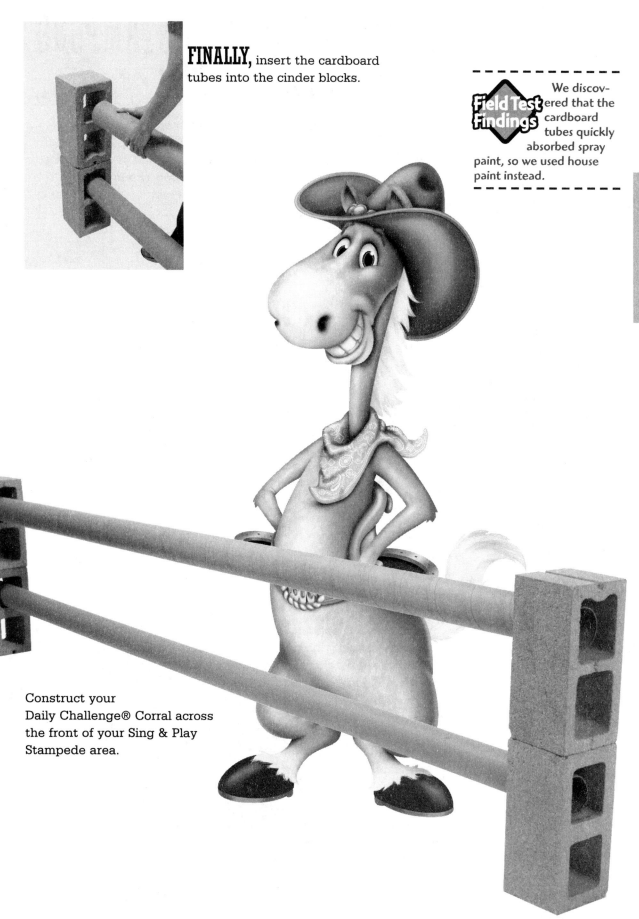

FINALLY, insert the cardboard tubes into the cinder blocks.

Construct your Daily Challenge® Corral across the front of your Sing & Play Stampede area.

BASICS

PRESCHOOLERS WILL STAMPEDE TO AVALANCHE RANCH

Preschoolers have a special Avalanche Ranch program of their own! Little adventurers join the older kids for opening and closing activities each day, and in between they enjoy fun, age-appropriate, Bible-learning activities in Prairie Dog Preschool. The Prairie Dog Preschool Director Manual contains complete instructions for setting up, organizing, and running Prairie Dog Preschool. Your Starter Kit includes leader manuals for the following preschool stations:

PRAIRIE DOG PRESCHOOL BIBLE ADVENTURES AND MISSIONS

Each day preschoolers experience an exciting Bible adventure in eye-catching, age-appropriate ways. They might march around the walls of Jericho or gather "stones" to build a memorial! Preschoolers will also discover how they can share God's love through Operation Kid-to-Kid. You'll love watching little ones work on their Operation Kid-to-Kid Prayer Bears!

PRAIRIE DOG PRESCHOOL CRAFT AND PLAY

Trail Tip Depending on which crafts you choose, preschoolers may make some of the same crafts as older kids. What a great way to help families remember each day's Bible Point together!

Preschoolers will explore the Bible story and daily Bible Point with all five senses through Prairie Dog Preschool Craft and Play. Here, preschoolers make crafts like Buddy Bags, Prayer Journals, Prayer Bears, Wild West Chalkboards, and Make-Your-Own Sheriff's Badges. They will also work in their Prairie Dog Bible Books and choose their Daily Challenges!

PRAIRIE DOG PRESCHOOL CHADDER'S THEATER

Your littlest learners will love a visit with Chadder! After watching the *Chadder's Wild West Adventure* DVD, preschoolers will explore the Treasure Verse through songs or activities and then receive a special Bible Memory Buddy.

Trail Tip

You may be tempted to have little ones rotate through the elementary Ranch Stations. Before you choose this option, please remember that early childhood education experts designed the field-tested activities in Prairie Dog Preschool—just for preschoolers! The activities in the elementary Ranch Stations were designed for—and tested by—elementary kids. Be sure to provide an age-appropriate program for preschoolers.

PRAIRIE DOG PRESCHOOL GAMES

Children continue their discoveries and work off some energy during Prairie Dog Preschool Games. These fun, energetic, and cooperative games reinforce the daily Bible Point and Bible story in exciting, memorable ways.

Preschoolers will stop in at Chuck Wagon Chow, too. One day, preschoolers even make a snack for the entire Avalanche Ranch VBS! What a *huge* accomplishment!

BASICS

MEET OUR BIBLE MEMORY BUDDIES!

Each day at Avalanche Ranch, kids meet an adorable buddy who reminds them of the day's Bible Point. They're Bible Memory Buddies®! We'll let our fun friends speak for themselves.

BASICS

It's me...Shadow! We ranch dogs stick close to the herd. That's an easy way to remind kids that God is with us.

Hi, partners! I'm Buc, the bucking bronco. I'm hopin' to let kids know that God is real!

Skye here. Eagles may be able to soar, but Jesus defeated death and rose from the tomb! I'll help kids discover that God is awesome.

My name's Boss! Longhorn cattle may look big and tough, but I know that God is in charge.

Hey, it's Ranger! I'm a big, strong bison, but God is bigger and stronger than anything. I want kids to know that God is strong.

To help kids remember these important Bible truths, the Chadder's Wild West Theater Leader will give each child a Bible Memory Buddy every day to keep in his or her Buddy Bag (an awesome craft that kids make on Day 1). And each Buddy has the Treasure Verse inscribed on it. Kids will *love* collecting these Buddies! And you'll be amazed at how the Bible Memory Buddies help kids apply Bible truths to everyday life.

BIBLE BASICS

Each day kids will be exposed to a Bible Point as well as to a corresponding Bible story and Treasure Verse. The chart below shows the Bible content kids will cover each day.

Day	Bible Point	Bible Story	Treasure Verse
1	God is real.	Rahab protects the Israelite spies (Joshua 2).	"The Lord is the only true God" (Jeremiah 10:10).
2	God is with us.	The Israelites cross the Jordan River (Joshua 3–4).	"For the Lord your God is with you wherever you go" (Joshua 1:9).
3	God is strong.	The walls of Jericho crash down (Joshua 6).	"The Lord is my strength" (Psalm 118:14).
4	God is awesome.	Jesus dies and rises again (Mark 15–16).	"For the Lord Most High is awesome" (Psalm 47:2).
5	God is in charge.	God heals Naaman (2 Kings 5).	"If you love me, obey my commandments" (John 14:15).

If you usually incorporate memory verses into your program, you can have kids memorize the daily Bible verses provided in this chart. Since children learn easy motions to each verse, it's a natural connection. Kids also collect the daily Bible Memory Buddies that have the daily Bible verses inscribed right on them! That makes learning the verse even more fun.

At each Ranch Station, kids will encounter a different presentation of the Bible Point, Bible story, or Bible verse.

"Wah-hoo!"

Field Test Findings At each station, kids will be carefully listening to hear the Bible Point so they can respond by shouting "Wah-hoo!" and waving their arms as if twirling a lasso. Watch their excitement and enthusiasm—and listening skills—build throughout the week.

- The Sing & Play Stampede Leader repeats the Bible Point each day.
- In addition to fun praise songs, kids sing at least one song each day that specifically ties to that day's Bible Point.
- Each day kids sing the Avalanche Ranch theme song, "Wild Ride!" which connects with the daily Bible Points.
- Each day the Sing & Play Stampede Leader summarizes the daily Bible story.

- The Cowpoke Crafts and Missions Leader repeats the Bible Point each day.
- Kids make Bible Point Crafts that remind them of each day's Bible story and Point. For example, a leather-bound Prayer Journal is a super way to remember that God hears our prayers because God is with us.
- Kids listen to the Sing & Play Stampede songs as they're working.
- The Cowpoke Crafts and Missions Leader asks questions to help kids review and apply the Bible Point and the Bible story.
- Through Operation Kid-to-Kid, kids experience what it means to share God's love.

- In each day's exciting cliffhanger video segment, Chadder Chipmunk explains the daily Bible Point.
- The Chadder's Wild West Theater Leader repeats the Bible Point each day.
- Kids read and explore key Bible verses to discover more about God and what it means to love and follow him. Then kids do exciting, memorable devotional activities to help them apply what they've learned about God to their daily lives.
- The Chadder's Wild West Theater Leader gives each child a Bible Memory Buddy inscribed with the day's Treasure Verse!

- The Chuck Wagon Chow Leader repeats the Bible Point each day.
- Kids make and eat snacks to reinforce the daily Bible Point. For example, on Day 4 kids make Awesome Avalanche Surprises. These ice cream sundae snacks remind kids that God is awesome.
- Kids show Jesus' love by serving others. Each day one set of Ranch Crews makes the snacks for the entire VBS—even the preschoolers get a chance to serve others!
- Kids listen to Sing & Play Stampede songs as they make and eat their snacks.

- The Horseplay Games Leader repeats the Bible Point each day.
- The Horseplay Games Leader acts as a "director" for Spotlight Drama™.

■ Kids play games that encourage them to apply what they've learned. For example, on Day 4, kids play Watering-Hole Relay, a game where they pass containers of water overhead. Kids discover how wonderful it is that God is awesome.

■ Kids listen to Sing & Play Stampede songs as they play games.

■ The games leader connects each game to the daily Bible Point.

Avalanche Ranch is soaring with Bible-based activities that will have kids flying high!

- The Wild Bible Adventures Leader repeats the Bible Point each day.
- Kids experience the daily Bible story in a hands-on way. For example, on Day 5 crew leaders rub smelly onion on kids' hands. Kids explore what it was like to have a disease that you *really* wanted to get rid of! They discover that God is in charge.

■ Ranch Crew Leaders guide small-group discussions in which kids connect their unforgettable Bible experiences to real life.

- The Showtime Roundup Leader repeats the Bible Point each day.
- Kids watch a Spotlight Drama, which reminds them of the daily Bible Point and Bible story.

■ Kids repeat the Sing & Play Stampede songs they've learned that day.

■ Kids use drama to apply what they've learned throughout the day and to remember the day's Treasure Verse. For example, on Day 2 kids act like the wild, wavy Jordan River and learn how God stopped the water from flowing so the Israelites could cross it.

- Preschoolers sing the Sing & Play Stampede songs with the older kids.
- Prairie Dog Preschool Leaders tell each day's Bible story in a fun, involving way.
- Prairie Dog Preschool Leaders repeat the Bible Point during each Craft and Play activity and game.

■ Preschoolers hear the Bible story and the Bible Point as they watch *Chadder's Wild West Adventure.*

■ Preschoolers work on interactive pages in their Prairie Dog Bible Books. These books are also filled with eye-catching pictures and preschool-friendly Daily Challenges to do at home.

■ Preschoolers make and eat snacks that reinforce the daily Bible story.

■ Preschoolers sing additional songs that reinforce the daily Bible Point or Bible story.

■ Preschoolers participate in Showtime Roundup with the older kids.

Trail Tip

On Day 1 only, preschoolers skip Sing & Play Stampede and go straight to Prairie Dog Preschool. This allows little ones to meet their preschool director, Ranch Crew Leaders, and Ranch Crew members. Plus, preschoolers get to make Chuck Wagon Chow snacks on Day 1, and the extra time helps them accomplish this big task.

RANCH STATIONS

At Avalanche Ranch, kids jump into Bible learning as they visit various Ranch Stations each day. Each station is staffed by an adult leader and features a different Bible-learning activity. Some stations— such as Sing & Play Stampede, Chuck Wagon Chow, and Showtime Roundup—accommodate all the Avalanche Ranch participants simultaneously. Kids will visit other stations in smaller groups.

Elementary-age kids visit the following stations each day:

- Sing & Play Stampede
- Cowpoke Crafts and Missions
- Horseplay Games
- Chuck Wagon Chow
- Chadder's Wild West Theater
- Wild Bible Adventures
- Showtime Roundup

Preschoolers spend most of their time in Prairie Dog Preschool, but they visit the following stations each day:

- Sing & Play Stampede
- Showtime Roundup

Preschoolers also enjoy the same Chuck Wagon Chow snacks *and* watch the same *Chadder's Wild West Adventure* video as the older children.

AVALANCHE RANCH FITS CHURCHES OF ALL SIZES

SMALL...

If you have fewer than 30 children, they can all explore the stations together.

This means that your station leaders will teach their areas only one time! (Station leaders may find this so easy that they will volunteer to teach more than one station, so you'll have fewer leaders to recruit!) Since you can set up multiple stations at one location, your church might be set up like this:

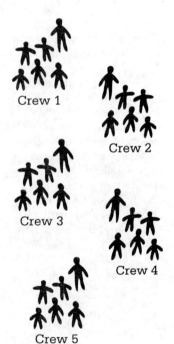

Crew 1

Crew 2

Crew 3

Crew 4

Crew 5

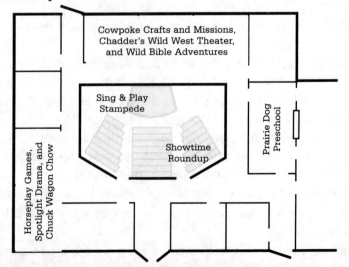

Cowpoke Crafts and Missions, Chadder's Wild West Theater, and Wild Bible Adventures

Sing & Play Stampede

Showtime Roundup

Prairie Dog Preschool

Horseplay Games, Spotlight Drama, and Chuck Wagon Chow

Your daily schedule might look as simple as this:

ALL CREWS

Sing & Play Stampede (9:00-9:25)

Allow five minutes to travel to your next station.

Wild Bible Adventures (9:30-9:50)

Allow five minutes to travel to your next station.

Cowpoke Crafts and Missions (9:55-10:15)

Allow five minutes to travel to your next station.

Chuck Wagon Chow (10:20-10:40)

Allow five minutes to travel to your next station.

Horseplay Games (10:45-11:05)

Allow five minutes to travel to your next station.

Chadder's Wild West Theater (11:10-11:30)

Allow five minutes to travel to your next station.

Showtime Roundup (11:35-12:00)

Trail Tip If you have kids rotating as one group, choose one crew each day that will skip games to make snacks for the rest of the VBS.

Field Test Findings We've heard from VBS directors who use this program and are delighted at how simple it is for smaller churches. Their leaders love teaching only one or two rotations, and it's easy to find leaders who will teach more than one. Your job has never been easier!

BASICS

MEDIUM...

If you have 50 to 150 kids at your Avalanche Ranch, you'll set up six stations, so your church might be set up like this:

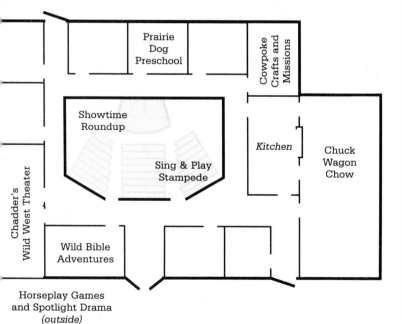

Divide your total number of elementary Ranch Crews by four to form four large groups.

These groups will travel to each station, following a schedule that looks like this:

TIME	GROUP A Crews 1-3	GROUP B Crews 4-6	GROUP C Crews 7-9	GROUP D Crews 10-12
9:00-9:25	Sing & Play Stampede	Sing & Play Stampede	Sing & Play Stampede	Sing & Play Stampede
Allow five minutes to travel to your next station.				
9:30-9:50	Wild Bible Adventures	Cowpoke Crafts and Missions	Chuck Wagon Chow Service	Chadder's Wild West Theater
Allow five minutes to travel to your next station.				
9:55-10:15	Cowpoke Crafts and Missions	Horseplay Games	Chadder's Wild West Theater	Wild Bible Adventures
Allow five minutes to travel to your next station.				
10:20-10:40	Chuck Wagon Chow	Chuck Wagon Chow	Chuck Wagon Chow	Chuck Wagon Chow
Allow five minutes to travel to your next station.				
10:45-11:05	Horseplay Games	Chadder's Wild West Theater	Wild Bible Adventures	Cowpoke Crafts and Missions
Allow five minutes to travel to your next station.				
11:10-11:30	Chadder's Wild West Theater	Wild Bible Adventures	Cowpoke Crafts and Missions	Horseplay Games
Allow five minutes to travel to your next station.				
11:35-12:00	Showtime Roundup	Showtime Roundup	Showtime Roundup	Showtime Roundup

LARGE!

If you have more than 150 kids, your church might be set up like this:

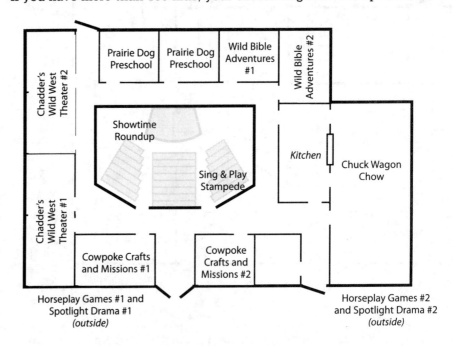

Trail Tip Don't worry if you need to set up duplicate stations—it's easy and really works best. If at all possible, place the duplicate stations next to each other. Then when Ranch Crews arrive at the stations, station leaders can simply direct half of them into each station.

Divide your total number of elementary Ranch Crews by eight to form eight large groups. These groups will travel to each Ranch Station, following a schedule that looks like this:

TIME	GROUP A Crews 1-4	GROUP B Crews 5-8	GROUP C Crews 9-12	GROUP D Crews 13-16
9:00-9:25	Sing & Play Stampede	Sing & Play Stampede	Sing & Play Stampede	Sing & Play Stampede
	Allow five minutes to travel to your next station.			
9:30-9:50	Wild Bible Adventures #1	Cowpoke Crafts and Missions #1	Chuck Wagon Chow Service	Chadder's Wild West Theater #1
	Allow five minutes to travel to your next station.			
9:55-10:15	Cowpoke Crafts and Missions #1	Horseplay Games #1	Chadder's Wild West Theater #1	Wild Bible Adventures #1
	Allow five minutes to travel to your next station.			
10:20-10:40	Chuck Wagon Chow	Chuck Wagon Chow	Chuck Wagon Chow	Chuck Wagon Chow
	Allow five minutes to travel to your next station.			
10:45-11:05	Horseplay Games #1	Chadder's Wild West Theater #1	Wild Bible Adventures #1	Cowpoke Crafts and Missions #1
	Allow five minutes to travel to your next station.			
11:10-11:30	Chadder's Wild West Theater #1	Wild Bible Adventures #1	Cowpoke Crafts and Missions #1	Horseplay Games #1
	Allow five minutes to travel to your next station.			
11:35-12:00	Showtime Roundup	Showtime Roundup	Showtime Roundup	Showtime Roundup

TIME	GROUP E Crews 17-20	GROUP F Crews 21-24	GROUP G Crews 25-28	GROUP H Crews 29-32
9:00-9:25	Sing & Play Stampede	Sing & Play Stampede	Sing & Play Stampede	Sing & Play Stampede
	Allow five minutes to travel to your next station.			
9:30-9:50	Wild Bible Adventures #2	Cowpoke Crafts and Missions #2	Chuck Wagon Chow Service	Chadder's Wild West Theater #2
	Allow five minutes to travel to your next station.			
9:55-10:15	Cowpoke Crafts and Missions #2	Horseplay Games #2	Chadder's Wild West Theater #2	Wild Bible Adventures #2
	Allow five minutes to travel to your next station.			
10:20-10:40	Chuck Wagon Chow	Chuck Wagon Chow	Chuck Wagon Chow	Chuck Wagon Chow
	Allow five minutes to travel to your next station.			
10:45-11:05	Horseplay Games #2	Chadder's Wild West Theater #2	Wild Bible Adventures #2	Cowpoke Crafts and Missions #2
	Allow five minutes to travel to your next station.			
11:10-11:30	Chadder's Wild West Theater #2	Wild Bible Adventures #2	Cowpoke Crafts and Missions #2	Horseplay Games #2
	Allow five minutes to travel to your next station.			
11:35-12:00	Showtime Roundup	Showtime Roundup	Showtime Roundup	Showtime Roundup

Field Test Findings VBS directors from large churches *love* the small-group crews and station-based format! Every child gets special attention from a loving crew leader, and the stations require the same amount of space...or even less!

Trail Tip For another large-group option, run a morning and evening program. Simply have participants sign up for the daytime or evening program; then decorate once and run two "shifts."

BASICS

RANCH CREWS

Field Test Findings

"Can't I just create crews of first- and second-graders, third- and fourth-graders, and so on?" Well, you could—but 12 years of experience has shown our team that this is *always* a bad idea. This VBS program is designed to succeed with kids of all ages working together. It's an amazing experience for kids—and adults! By forming age-graded crews, you create a wealth of problems and rob kids of a new and memorable experience.

Field Test Findings

Try to structure your crews so that they contain no more than six members. Through field-testing and customer feedback, we've discovered that larger crews can get unmanageable and become a frustration for the crew leaders—and the kids. Plus, smaller crews maximize important relationship-building time in the crew.

Trail Tip

Be sure to distribute the Crew Leader Pocket Guide to all crew leaders during your leader training time. Have extras available at Avalanche Ranch for crew leaders who are unable to attend leader training. These guidebooks contain discussion questions, tips, and follow-up ideas for your leaders.

ELEMENTARY CREW LEADER POCKET GUIDE

As you set up your Avalanche Ranch, you will assign kids to Ranch Crews. On Day 1 kids report to their Ranch Crews right away to start getting acquainted. Ranch Crews encourage kids to make new friends because Ranch Crew members work closely with each other all week at VBS. They also provide an organizational structure that helps kids progress from station to station in an orderly manner.

Ranch Crews consist of three to five children and an adult or teenage Ranch Crew Leader. To keep Ranch Crews manageable, it's a good idea to assign three children to each Ranch Crew. Then encourage children to invite their friends to fill up their crews. If possible, assign one child from each age level to each crew. "Your Ranch Crew 'Family' " (p. 31) highlights the unique contribution children from each age level can make to a Ranch Crew. The "Who's Who on the Crew?" chart on page 33 lists the five jobs elementary Ranch Crew members may fill during Avalanche Ranch.

Preschoolers' Ranch Crews consist of up to five preschoolers and an adult or teenage crew leader.

Detailed instructions for setting up Ranch Crews begin on page 156. Qualifications for crew leaders are listed on page 103.

YOUR RANCH CREW "FAMILY"

...ust finished fifth grade. I'm ...unique and important part ...my Ranch Crew because ...ike to make choices. I can ...lp my Ranch Crew make ...oices about a crew name, ...bs, and activities.

I just finished fourth grade. I'm a unique and important part of my Ranch Crew because I like to ask questions. I can help my Ranch Crew ask questions to make sure we understand what we're learning.

I just finished third grade. I'm a unique and important part of my Ranch Crew because I like to be challenged. I can help younger members of my Ranch Crew with challenging projects.

...t finished second ...e. I'm a unique ...important part ...y Ranch Crew ...use I want ...ything to be fair. I ...help make sure we ...ke turns and treat ...another fairly.

I just finished first grade. I'm a unique and important part of my Ranch Crew because I like to be the best. I can help encourage my Ranch Crew to be the best it can be.

I just finished kindergarten. I'm a unique and important part of my Ranch Crew because I have a great imagination. I can help my Ranch Crew pretend we're really visiting a ranch!

WORKING WITH MIXED-AGE CREWS

You may be skeptical about placing kids in mixed-age groups. After all, that's probably not how your other children's ministry functions are structured. And the school system is set up to be age-graded, too. So why should you shake things up and try combining ages? Here's why!

Combined-age Ranch Crews encourage teamwork rather than competition. When kids are grouped in age-graded classes, there's more emphasis on comparison ("I can do it better!") and competition ("I can do it faster!"). However, by placing children in mixed-age crews, you nearly eliminate the unspoken desire for kids to compare or compete. Instead, older kids help younger ones with challenging tasks. Younger kids seek to emulate the older, "cool" kids in their crews.

Combined-age Ranch Crews reduce discipline problems. Now we *love* kids of all ages, but there's something intimidating about that group of fifth-grade boys. But when you split up that daunting bunch of preteen kids, they suddenly lose their "audience" (that is, one another), and your discipline problems nearly vanish. You'll get the same delightful effect when you split up middle-elementary cliques, some siblings, and other "troublesome twosomes." It works!

Combined-age Ranch Crews encourage relationship-building. By mixing ages to form small groups, you provide a rare opportunity for kids of all ages to get to know one another. Most kids in your community are with one another during school, sports, and other children's ministry functions. Multi-age Ranch Crews give kids the chance to interact and build meaningful relationships with new friends.

Combined-age Ranch Crews are easier to work with. Your Ranch Crew Leaders will *love* how easy it is to work with kids of mixed ages. Rather than trying to assist a group of 6-year-olds with reading or crafts, a crew leader can give one-on-one attention to one 6-year-old. And (believe it or not) older kids will relish their helping role as they lead with their strengths.

There are countless reasons mixed-age crews truly are more effective than age-graded crews. But don't take our word for it! Log on to www.group.com/vbs, and ask other directors who have tried this method.

DID YOU KNOW?

Studies show that children learn as much—or more—when they're linked with kids of different ages. In fact, one study observed that children naturally chose to play with other children their age only 6 percent of the time. They played with children at least one year older or younger 55 percent of the time.

EVERYONE HAS A JOB!

During Sing & Play Stampede on Day 1, kids choose Ranch Crew jobs. You can expect each of the following jobs to be represented in each Ranch Crew. If crews have fewer than five kids, some kids may have more than one job.

In addition to the five jobs listed below, each crew should have an adult or teenage Ranch Crew Leader. You can count on the crew leader to help kids complete the activities at each station.

Kids are excited about having special jobs! Each leader manual suggests ways station leaders can call on kids to fulfill the job responsibilities they've chosen.

WHO'S WHO ON THE CREW?

JOBS	DUTIES
READER	■ likes to read ■ reads Bible passages aloud
RANCH GUIDE	■ chooses action ideas for traveling between stations (such as tiptoeing, hopping, galloping, or marching) ■ helps monitor the daily schedule to let the Ranch Crew know what's coming next
MATERIALS MANAGER	■ likes to distribute and collect supplies ■ distributes and collects Wild Ride Bible Guides ■ carries the crew's bag until the day is over
COACH	■ likes to smile and make people happy ■ makes sure people use kind words and actions ■ leads group in cheering during Horseplay Games
PRAYER PERSON	■ likes to pray and isn't afraid to pray aloud ■ makes sure the group takes time to pray each day ■ leads or opens prayer times

Field Test Findings As VBS director, you'll find that open, clear communication is your best friend! Be sure to touch base with the Sing & Play Stampede Leader to remind him or her to allow time for children to choose their roles on Day 1. Although this process is written into the Sing & Play Stampede Leader Manual, it's good to double-check and be sure the leader understands the importance of this process.

Trail Tip Each Ranch Crew will need one Crew Bag in which to carry its Wild Ride Bible Guides, Bible Memory Buddies, and Bible Point Crafts. Crew Bags are available from Group Publishing and your local Group supplier.

MIDDLE SCHOOLERS

Field Test Findings

When we used sixth-graders as assistant crew leaders, we learned that, depending on interests and maturity level, some were interested in doing the crafts, games, and snacks as participants rather than being crew leaders. Use your best judgment as each situation arises. We've learned to order a few extra crafts so they can get in on the fun, too.

Field Test Findings

It's important that middle school kids understand the specifics of their jobs. We discovered that assigning kids this age to be "floaters," who could fill in wherever there were needs, gave them too much freedom and not enough direction. When we gave them specific roles, such as Assistant Chef or Assistant Cowpoke Crafts Leader, they did super jobs to help us out!

Trail Tip

Make sure you choose more mature fifth- and sixth-graders for leadership roles. Many kids this age still enjoy being crew members and participating in all activities. Some upper-elementary kids will feel left out if they can't make their own crafts or participate fully in other activities. Be sure to ask kids what *they* would like to do instead of assuming they would rather "opt out."

Many churches are unsure how to handle middle school kids; they seem too old for some children's ministry programs and too young for youth group. With Avalanche Ranch, middle school kids can fill a number of roles. (In fact, middle schoolers at our field test reported that they loved helping because it gave them the chance to be adults *and* kids.) Check out the following options to find the perfect fit for your middle schoolers. They can

■ **join Ranch Crews as Assistant Ranch Crew Leaders.** Many middle schoolers are ready for simple leadership roles, but they still enjoy participating in activities such as games, snack times, crafts, and biblical dramas. As Assistant Ranch Crew Leaders, they can help their crew leaders by keeping kids together, working with younger children during Cowpoke Crafts, or doing the more difficult jobs during Chuck Wagon Chow Service.

■ **become assistant station leaders.** Your middle schoolers are developing their gifts and talents and are discovering the things they excel at and enjoy. Being an assistant station leader is a great way to encourage kids toward this discovery. Do you know an older child who's developing a love for drama and storytelling? Use him or her as an Assistant Showtime Roundup Leader or an Assistant Wild Bible Adventures Leader. What about a child who enjoys sports and other athletic activities? Ask him or her to be an Assistant Horseplay Games Leader. Your station leaders will love the extra help, and older kids will enjoy the added responsibility.

■ **help with Prairie Dog Preschool registration.** Some middle schoolers are nurturing and caring—great qualities for helping preschoolers find their way at Avalanche Ranch. For the first day or two, have a few middle schoolers available to act as guides, helping preschoolers find their Ranch Crew Leaders, showing preschoolers the restrooms, or playing with shy children to get them accustomed to the Prairie Dog Preschool area.

■ **create a Singalong Crew.** Older children (who might normally hesitate to sing and move to music) will enjoy teaching song motions and leading younger children in Sing & Play Stampede. Ask a group of middle school kids to work with the Sing & Play Stampede Leader to learn the words and motions to all Avalanche Ranch songs. The Singalong Crew will add visual excitement and energy to your singing time.

Middle schoolers have so much to offer (and gain from) your program! We've heard countless stories of middle schoolers and teenagers whose lives were changed because of their experiences in leading or assisting in VBS. The more these kids are involved in your program, the more opportunities you have to touch their lives.

TEENAGERS

Teenagers have an important role in making Avalanche Ranch a success! Use the following suggestions to involve teenagers (or college students) in your program.

- **Have them act as Ranch Crew Leaders.** Many young adults have younger siblings or baby-sit frequently and are comfortable working with children. Young adults will have a great time leading their crews—and will love how easy it is. (Teenagers will actually get as much out of the Bible stories and discussions as the young children will!)

- **Let teenagers and young adults help with registration.** Many young people have excellent organizational skills. These young people enjoy forming crews, greeting children, and helping kids find their Ranch Crew Leaders. (These helpers make a great first impression for adults as well as kids.) After the first day, your registration helpers can register newcomers, count the daily attendance and report the number to the Chuck Wagon Chow Leader, and fill in for crew leaders who are absent.

- **Have qualified teenagers run your sound system or act as Spotlight Drama photographers.** Some high school drama programs train young people to run sound, lighting, and video equipment. These teenagers make excellent Avalanche Ranch technical staff members.

- **Ask teenagers to act as Bible characters.** The Wild Bible Adventures Leader needs a few volunteers to act as Bible characters in simple dramas. Teenagers with dramatic flair enjoy playing Rowdy in Sing & Play Stampede or the Sergeant in Wild Bible Adventures.

- **If your church's youth group has a choir or worship band, let it help with Sing & Play Stampede and Showtime Roundup.** Kids at Avalanche Ranch love singing with the "big kids," and young adults will never have such a receptive and friendly audience again. Your station leaders enjoy the extra backup and enthusiasm. Plus, teenagers learn and grow right along with the children!

There are countless ways to involve youth in Avalanche Ranch. Just let teenagers find roles where their gifts, talents, or interests lead them. You'll be surprised at how committed and enthusiastic these young volunteers are.

Field Test Findings Who says VBS is just for little kids? We've heard so many stories of how teenagers' lives were touched by past VBS programs. Young adults who volunteered had such a great time and were so moved by the Bible experiences that they made life-changing decisions!

Field Test Findings Let your teenagers get involved. We've heard from churches that allowed their youth to choose the material and then run the entire program as their summer outreach or service project. They discovered that it's a super way to involve young people in real hands-on ministry.

Trail Tip If you're used to having a class for youth (and have all the volunteers you need), now there's a resource to help you out! The Wild Ride Youth Leader Manual allows middle schoolers and high schoolers to participate in Sing & Play Stampede and then attend their own special class. Teenagers come back for the closing Showtime Roundup, so everyone can get in on the fun. The Wild Ride Youth Leader Manual is available from Group Publishing or your local Group supplier.

WILD RIDE BIBLE GUIDES

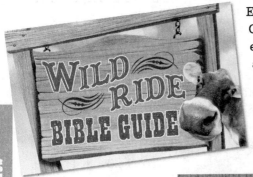

Each child at Avalanche Ranch will need a Wild Ride Bible Guide. The Bible Guide includes faith-stretching questions, eye-catching devotional activities, two cool sticker sheets, and Daily Challenges that kids will wear home each day. While traditional student pages are filled with pointless puzzles and word searches, the Wild Ride Bible Guide allows kids to explore God's Word in unforgettable ways, apply it to their lives, and share their excitement with friends and family.

Preschoolers have their own age-appropriate Prairie Dog Bible Books, complete with age-appropriate family activities, colorful stickers, and five activity pages to make Bible learning fun and memorable at VBS. Even preschoolers enjoy *this* wild ride through God's Word!

And don't forget Operation Kid-to-Kid! Each Bible Guide (for elementary *and* preschool) includes a copy of *The Survivor's Bible* booklet written in French. These books will help at-risk kids in South and Central Africa.

Kids at Avalanche Ranch will write or draw messages of God's love inside these books. Then they'll present the books and Prayer Bears as an offering, to be sent to kids in Africa. Missions just don't get any easier than this!

CHADDER CHIPMUNK™

Chadder Chipmunk is a lovable, mischievous character the kids love. Each day when kids visit Chadder's Wild West Theater, they view a segment of *Chadder's Wild West Adventure*.

Chadder arrives at the Horsefeathers Dude Ranch, excited to become a real cowboy—just like his great grandfather, Chester Chipmunk. Unfortunately, Chadder has a hard time finding a horse (or any other animal) to ride. During the cattle roundup, Chadder rides with Calamity Jean, the ranch cook, who doesn't believe in God. They get tricked by a cattle rustler named Snake and his silly sidekick Miss Kittycat, survive a thunderstorm, almost fall off the edge of a cliff, and eat way too many M&M's candies. It's a wild ride, but Chadder and his friends all discover that God loves us.

The Chadder's Wild West Theater Leader Manual contains discussion questions and powerful hands-on devotions that go along with each day's segment of *Chadder's Wild West Adventure*. The DVD is available from Group Publishing and your local Group supplier.

Field Test Findings

Each year at our field test, kids can't wait to see each day's adventure! The continuing drama, comical characters, and cliffhanger endings build great anticipation and keep kids coming back for more each day.

Field Test Findings

You might be tempted to have kids watch the Chadder video while eating their snacks, omitting the debriefing time that surrounds the video. *Don't give in to temptation!* These activities and questions are carefully crafted to help kids discover and apply God's Word to real life. By skipping these activities, you'll rob kids of *powerful* experiences—ones that can even be life-changing! Our crew leaders often left the Chadder station with tears still flowing from the heart-tugging activities they had done with their kids.

BIBLE POINT CRAFTS

OK, you're right—every VBS program includes crafts. (And you probably have a few crafty folks at your church who could pull together some nifty projects on their own.) So what makes these crafts so special?

Each Bible Point Craft connects with the Bible story and Bible Point. Now *that's* different! Everything at Avalanche Ranch ties together to reinforce one simple, memorable Bible Point—and crafts are no exception. These crafts not only tie in to the western theme but also will be lasting mementos of important *Bible* truths.

Bible Point Crafts are child-tested and irresistible. No need for

your kids to be guinea pigs for what you *think* they will like. We've tested these crafts in a real VBS setting! We asked kids what they liked about the crafts, listened to kids' conversations as they worked on the crafts, and watched what kids did with the crafts during (and after) Avalanche Ranch. These are *all* child-pleasers—even for those hard-to-please fifth-grade boys!

Bible Point Crafts allow for lots of creativity. Don't let these easy craft kits fool you. They're easy for you, *and* they allow kids plenty of options for creativity and self-expression. We know because we've seen what kids can do with these crafts. Prepare to be dazzled by your kids' creativity!

Bible Point Crafts are downright fun! You may run across crafts that look adorable when they're finished—but all they do is hang on a refrigerator or sit on a shelf. Forget those boring pencil holders, doorknob danglers, or paperweights. Kids are active, so we figure that their crafts should be, too! Kids will definitely be wild for *these* craft "toys" that zip, snuggle, draw, and connect!

Bible Point Crafts are "doable." Flip through some craft magazines, and you'll be amazed at the crafts they tout as "child-friendly." (At least, they're not friendly to many kids *we* know!) Since groups of *real* kids have tested these crafts, we know that these projects won't frustrate or bore the kids at Avalanche Ranch. And the crafts are relatively no-mess, so you don't have to wait for the glue or paint to dry overnight. Kids can use and play with these amazing crafts right away!

Bible Point Crafts are exclusive. These keepsakes are available only with our special VBS. That means you'll delight and surprise kids with these unique projects they can get nowhere else! Kids will be excited about getting their hands on these never-been-done crafts.

Bible Point Crafts give you more options. VBS directors and craft station leaders asked us to provide more options so they could choose the best crafts for their particular church setting, so now you have two choices for each day. Can't decide which to do? Then do them all! Just purchase extra craft options to use at summer Sunday school, children's church, day camp, family camp, or midweek programs. Or save them for the fall to use for other special children's ministry events.

Bible Point Crafts are cost-effective. Whatever your budget, there's something for you in this manual. On a tight budget? Stretch your VBS dollars with Group's Fund-Your-VBS Kit, included in your Starter Kit. And since kids make keepsake reminders of the Bible truths they've learned, you know that these crafts won't end up in the trash. You'll be using your dollars wisely!

At our field test, we watched and timed kids *very closely* to make sure each craft could be finished in the allotted time. By the time we got kids in the room, settled down, explained the craft, and distributed supplies, only 15 minutes remained for kids to work on their crafts (which was *plenty* of time to finish these easy crafts). Plus, your craft leader will need some time each day to talk about Operation Kid-to-Kid. Allow kids the time to be creative on their crafts (and to play with these irresistible toys!). You'll be delighted at what you see.

COOPERATION, *NOT* COMPETITION

At Avalanche Ranch, you'll have highly competitive kids and kids who hate competing, athletic kids and couch-potato kids, kids who are used to winning and kids who have never once crossed the finish line first.

That means you'll have to help your kids break the "competition habit." Whether it's games, singing, devotions, or mission offerings, your goal is for kids to work *with* one another, not *against* one another. It's a new concept for some of your kids.

These quick tips will help:

1. Remember, relationships first.
The purpose of Avalanche Ranch is to help kids grow in their faith and to encourage healthy relationships. Ten years from now, nobody will remember who won the relay race or who brought more kids to VBS, but friendships made at Avalanche Ranch can continue to be a blessing.

2. Call on kids by their Ranch Crew roles.
Each day, kids will choose a different role to play within their Ranch Crews. Kids might be a Reader, Prayer Person, Coach, Materials Manager, or Ranch Guide. Crew roles help kids feel important and purposeful—they really do like having a special job each day!

3. Create an environment in which everyone succeeds.
Why create a competitive environment that ensures *someone* will walk away a loser? You may be used to having kids earn prizes for Bible memory, but consider how a visitor might feel if he or she doesn't earn the prize. Are "boys versus girls" penny drives usually part of your VBS? Think about having a missons project where you can celebrate everyone's achievements.

4 Don't allow put-downs.
Set this as a clear expectation, and *enforce* it. Your kids will grow in their faith as they see that cooperation, not competition, creates a servant heart.

5 Applaud effort, not accomplishment.
Encourage constantly. Be lavish with applause. Make it fun for kids to try new things, even if they fail. Build kids up!

6 Check your own "competition meter."
Do you get caught up in competition? love winning at all costs? If so, realize that you must model cooperation if you expect kids to do it. The cooperative spirit of your VBS begins with you.

7 Pray, pray, pray.
Pray that God will use your VBS to draw kids and their leaders closer to him and to one another.

Trail Tip
Where is competition creeping into your VBS? We've seen churches turn worship (who can sing the loudest), missions (who can bring in the most money), outreach (who can bring the most visitors), and even God's Word (who can learn the most Bible verses) into a competition. We urge you to think *carefully* before assuming that competition is the best motivator. How did Jesus motivate his followers? How can we fashion our ministry after that of Jesus?

BASICS

Field Test Findings
We've discovered that kids truly can have as much fun (if not more) with cooperative activities. And everyone gets to participate and succeed!

NOW GET OUT THERE AND GET READY TO HAVE SOME FUN!

KIDS *REALLY CAN* MAKE THEIR OWN SNACKS

Each day at Avalanche Ranch, a different group of kids skips its Horseplay Games time to prepare snacks for the entire VBS. Snack preparation provides kids with a unique opportunity to live out the daily Bible Point by serving others. And it makes your job easier because you don't have to recruit additional volunteers to make snacks. (Some churches have said snack preparation was the biggest hurdle to overcome. But after letting kids try it, snack preparation became one of the best parts of their VBS experience.)

Believe it or not, one-fourth of your kids *can* prepare snacks for everyone else—if you follow the field-tested, step-by-step instructions provided in the Chuck Wagon Chow Leader Manual. Each day snack preparation will follow the simple procedures outlined below.

1. Before kids arrive, the Chuck Wagon Chow Leader sets out supplies according to the instructions provided in the Chuck Wagon Chow Leader Manual.

2. After kids arrive and wash their hands, the leader explains each step of the snack preparation and invites kids to choose which steps they would like to work on.

3. Kids work in assembly lines to prepare the snacks. Ranch Crew Leaders are assigned the more difficult tasks, such as handling sharp knives or pouring drinks.

4. Kids set out the completed snacks on tables, where they will be picked up and gobbled down during Chuck Wagon Chow.

Trail Tip

Of course it sounds simpler to just distribute cookies and juice at snack time. But isn't it worth a little extra effort to give kids the opportunity to actually serve others? You'll be amazed to see children working together, and the kids will be delighted to see what a big job they can accomplish. Don't rob them of a valuable (and fun) learning and serving experience.

Field Test Findings

"Kids won't want to give up their game time to make snacks." Think again! Friends tell us that snack service is something kids *really* look forward to. We think it's terrific that kids look forward to serving others.

SPY GUY TRAIL MIX

STICK WITH US S'MORES

BASICS

TUMBLING JERICHO WALLS

AWESOME AVALANCHE SURPRISE

NAAMAN'S DIP

Kids who serve on the Chuck Wagon Chow Service Crew report for snack preparation right after Sing & Play Stampede. They will take 20 to 25 minutes to prepare snacks before moving on to their next station. And just in case kids don't finish in time, the Chuck Wagon Chow Leader has an additional 20 to 25 minutes to make final preparations before all the children arrive to eat. In Avalanche Ranch field tests, even preschoolers were able to complete their snack preparation within the allotted time.

As director, you'll want to drop in on the Chuck Wagon Chow Service Crew each day. Ask the leader how kids' work is progressing, and affirm the children for a job well done. But don't linger too long; you may distract kids from completing their work. Be sure to return at snack time to see children explain the meaning of the snack as *they* teach the Bible Point. Then watch the Chuck Wagon Chow Service Crew kids' faces light up as they're recognized for their accomplishment.

Field Test Findings A VBS director who participated in our field test admitted that he had never let the kids create the snacks. After seeing how doable (and downright fun) it was, he was sold!

SPOTLIGHT DRAMA

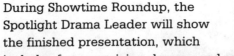
With Spotlight Dramas, every child at Avalanche Ranch can be a star. Here's how it works:

Each day, a different group of kids will arrive at Horseplay Games to discover that a photographer (the Spotlight Drama Leader) is there to capture cool photos of them for a custom PowerPoint slide show. The daily schedules in the Spotlight Drama Leader Manual explain which group is featured each day—but for kids, it's a surprise! The Spotlight Drama Leader Manual includes a script, outlining the specific shots to get. The Horseplay Games Leader energizes kids, acting as a director who gets kids into poses, and allows the photographer to focus on getting amazing shots.

When the "photo session" is finished (it takes only about 10 minutes), the kids head off with the Horseplay Games Leader for a few games. Then the Spotlight Drama Leader has more than an hour until Showtime Roundup to copy the photo files from the camera to the computer and insert them into the PowerPoint show for that day. It's *that* easy!

During Showtime Roundup, the Spotlight Drama Leader will show the finished presentation, which includes fun, surprising dramas and sound effects.

This hands-on mission project allows kids to reach around the world with God's love!

WHAT IS OPERATION KID-TO-KID™?

MORE THAN AN OFFERING

You may be used to having children bring money as a missions offering. However, most children don't understand the value of money—it's not a tangible "need" for them. That makes it difficult for them to make a concrete connection between their money and really making a difference in the life of another child.

Trail Tip

One of our team members recalled a time the kids at her VBS raised money to buy a cow for a needy family overseas. Each day the leaders tallied the coins and announced the money kids had raised. At the end of the week, the VBS director proudly declared the grand total...and the room was silent. The kids were unimpressed with a dollar amount—they really just wanted to see the actual cow they had "bought."

On the other hand, children *are* familiar with stuffed animals. As most parents in North America will tell you, kids have mountains of cuddly animals propped up on their beds. So kids definitely feel empathy for children who don't have a special stuffed animal to snuggle with at night.

That's why we developed Operation Kid-to-Kid! Over the years, Operation Kid-to-Kid has become one of the world's largest child-to-child service outreach programs! We've designed this missions project to have a big impact—on the kids who give *and* on the kids who receive!

Trail Tip

Today's kids are service-minded and want to make a difference, both globally and within their communities.

THE GREATEST GIFT

International Bible Society believes that children are of strategic importance to the church. Research consistently indicates that the majority of those who make a commitment to Christ do so between the ages of 4 and 14. The vision of IBS is to change the hearts of today's generation to change tomorrow's world. One of their outreach efforts is to at-risk children in Africa.

There are a staggering number of orphans in Africa—many of them left alone because of the AIDS epidemic. That's why IBS partners with many missions organizations, with the goal of serving and ministering to children in such hopeless, desperate situations.

Operation Kid-to-Kid™ is an international missions project that allows hundreds of thousands of kids in North America to serve children around the world!

By partnering with International Bible Society, we want to give the kids at Avalanche Ranch the opportunity to share God's love. The kids at your VBS will make two Operation Kid-to-Kid Prayer Bears—cuddly, snuggly, adorable little bears that say "Jesus" in English, French, and Spanish. Kids will keep one bear as a reminder to pray for the African child who receives the other bear. Kids will also give a special copy of *The Survivor's Bible* booklet (in French) as a way to help at-risk children discover God's love.

> **Nearly 34 million orphans live in the continent of Africa. That's approximately the population of California.**

Just think: When your church participates, you'll join other Avalanche Ranch VBS programs, and together you could contribute more than *one million* Scripture books and teddy bears to needy children! Operation Kid-to-Kid is a practical, meaningful way for kids to demonstrate Jesus' love through giving and service. (For more information about the impact of Operation Kid-to-Kid, check out www.ok2k.org.)

HOW YOUR KIDS CAN HELP

Each child will find a copy of a booklet titled *Les Survivant* inside his or her Wild Ride Bible Guide. (We'll call it *The Survivor's Bible* to make it easy.) But this powerful Scripture book isn't all! You will purchase enough Operation Kid-to-Kid Prayer Bears so each child has two. On Day 3, kids will make their bears, and then draw a picture or write a note inside the front cover of *The Survivor's Bible*. Kids can also slip a note into the bear's pocket as a constant reminder of God's love. Then crews will join hands and pray for the children who receive the teddy bears and books. Children will keep their Prayer Bears in the Crew Bag until the end of the week.

During Showtime Roundup on Day 5, each child will present one bear as an offering, along with a copy of *The Survivor's Bible*. This is a powerful, moving ceremony. Kids and leaders will be amazed as they see just how many bears and books they can send to Africa. It's a concrete way for kids to see that it's easy to spread God's love. (And it's just one more way to add to their Daily Challenge accomplishments.)

IT'S AS EASY AS 1, 2, 3!

1. On Day 1, the Cowpoke Crafts and Missions Leader will show the Operation Kid-to-Kid segment of the *Wah-hoo!* DVD. This three-minute clip is a moving way to get everyone excited about sharing God's love! The Cowpoke Crafts Leader will explain the importance of *The Survivor's Bible* and bears and remind kids that they can help others with this easy program.

Trail Tip Let your whole church in on the action! In the entryway of your church, set out several completed Operation Kid-to-Kid Prayer Bears. Include a sign-up sheet for people to sign up and make one themselves. Invite families, women's groups, youth groups, the missions board, *everyone* in your church to join the Operation Kid-to-Kid easy missions project. Think of how many people your entire church might touch with the warmth of God's love!

OPERATION KID-TO-KID

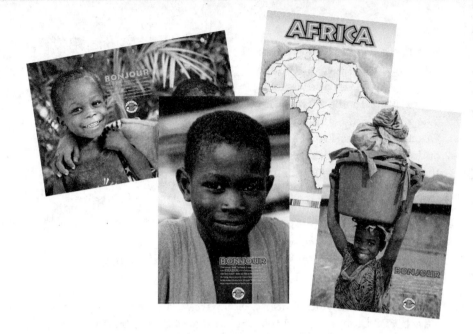

These bears *really* were a meaningful gift from kids. We originally had kids only make one bear to give away, but many kids struggled with giving up their treasured teddy. Some kids wanted a bear to keep as a reminder to pray for the person who had the other bear. Plan on providing two bears—to avoid tears *and* to give kids something to use as a "prayer spark" for months to come!

Even preschoolers got in on this easy missions project. They create bears and color a "picture" in their copy of *The Survivor's Bible.* What a precious opportunity for your youngest learners to give something from the heart!

Throughout the week, the Cowpoke Crafts and Missions Leader will also hang up a new Operation Kid-to-Kid poster each day. The kids at your Avalanche Ranch VBS will *love* seeing the faces and hearing the stories of kids who may receive these gifts of love. (Operation Kid-to-Kid posters are available from Group Publishing or your local Group VBS supplier.)

2. On Day 3, the Cowpoke Crafts Leader will distribute two Prayer Bears to each child. Kids will gently stuff the bears with Poly-Fil, comparing the stuffing to how they're filling children's lives with God's love. They'll add felt hearts inside the bears and then seal the bears. Each child will write or draw a special note in the front of his or her copy of *The Survivor's Bible* as a message to the recipient. Finally, children will place a note in the bear's pocket. Each crew will huddle and pray for the children who will receive their gifts of love.

3. On Day 5, during Showtime Roundup, kids will each come forward and set their Prayer Bears and copies of *The Survivor's Bible* on the stage as an offering.

AND *YOUR* JOB IS EASY, TOO!

After your Avalanche Ranch ends, it's time to send your Prayer Bears and Bible books to International Bible Society for distribution. Follow these simple steps to ensure that your items will be a special part of this world-changing project.

1. Look over each bear to be sure it is finished and securely sealed.

2. Place the bears and books in a sturdy box. Please include a check for $25 (made out to International Bible Society) to help cover distribution and ministry costs.

3. Seal the box, and mail it to:

> International Bible Society
> c/o Operation Kid-to-Kid
> 1820 Jet Stream Drive
> Colorado Springs, CO 80921

Thanks for joining us in this exciting, world-changing project!

WOW! LOOK WHAT KIDS HAVE DONE THROUGH OPERATION KID-TO-KID™!

- **1998** Kids in North America sent more than 91,000 school supply kits to children around the world.

- **1999** Children involved in Operation Kid-to-Kid sent approximately 400,000 Spanish translations of the Gospel of John to Spanish-speaking children around the world.

- **2000** Film Crews at Group's HolyWord Studios created more than 100,000 Care Kits that were distributed in countries such as Thailand, Vietnam, and Albania.

- **2001** Cool Crews who took part in Polar Expedition sent more than 380,000 Gift Boxes to needy children across the globe!

- **2002** It's estimated that children in North America sent more than one million Bible coloring books to orphans in Russia and Romania! Wow!

- **2003** Kids at Group's SCUBA VBS sent more than 310,000 pairs of shoes and over 200,000 pairs of socks to orphans around the world. (We think that's *shoe*-per!)

- **2004** More than 1.5 million Spanish-speaking kids received Spanish Bible books from children at Lava Lava Island.

- **2005** Kids at Serengeti Trek sent more than one million Bible books and hundreds of thousands of school supply kits to needy children in Africa.

- **2006** We blanketed the world with Jesus' love! Kids, youth, and adults participating in Fiesta sent approximately 250,000 "Jesus Loves Me" blankets to children in Latin American countries.

PLANNING FOR OPERATION KID-TO-KID™

BEFORE AVALANCHE RANCH

■ **Inform your congregation.** Let your congregation know that the kids in your church will be sending teddy bears to orphans in Africa. Photocopy the "Bearing Gifts of Love!" flier (p. 52), and distribute it at a worship service.

■ **Involve your congregation.** Church members can help by sponsoring a bear or even by making additional bears themselves. This is a wonderful project that can involve the entire congregation!

✔ Use the Fund-Your-VBS Kit (found in your Avalanche Ranch Starter Kit) to raise additional funds to purchase the special Prayer Bears and copies of *The Survivor's Bible*. Remember, the kids who receive these gifts will be reminded of Jesus' love *every* time they hug their bears!

✔ Check with your college group, singles group, or senior citizens group to see if they would be interested in making Prayer Bears.

✔ Take a special offering to collect money to buy the special bears. If each child brings $1, you'll more than cover the cost of this outreach program. You can also use additional funds for shipping charges.

✔ Ask about shipping discounts. Many shipping companies offer deep discounts to employees and family members. Check to see if anyone in your congregation can get such a discount toward shipping the Prayer Bears to IBS.

■ **Inform your community.** Photocopy the "Operation Kid-to-Kid™ News Release" (p. 53), and fill in the information regarding your church's program. Send the news release to local newspapers, television stations, and radio stations (especially your Christian radio station) so they can let others in your community know about your participation in Operation Kid-to-Kid.

■ **Distribute Operation Kid-to-Kid posters.** Give the Operation Kid-to-Kid posters to the Prairie Dog Preschool Director and the Cowpoke Crafts and Missions Leader. This poster set includes a map of Africa and colorful posters of three children who are representative of those who will receive the books and bears.

Field Test Findings

We hear from countless churches that make Operation Kid-to-Kid a community service project or send the items with a church missions team. Remember, Operation Kid-to-Kid is *flexible*—that's why so many people make it an integral part of their VBS!

Trail Tip

Operation Kid-to-Kid intentionally involves several different stations so it becomes an integral part of Avalanche Ranch. Be sure to communicate with crew leaders, the Cowpoke Crafts and Missions Leader, and the Showtime Roundup Leader so everyone understands his or her role in this awesome project.

OPERATION KID-TO-KID

DURING AVALANCHE RANCH

- **Affirm kids when they accomplish their mission.** Each day, lead kids in cheering and celebrating the big, world-changing job they're doing.

- **Check in with Ranch Crew Leaders.** During your opening huddle and prayer with the Ranch Crew Leaders, ask them how kids are doing on the Operation Kid-to-Kid Prayer Bears.

- **Encourage kids to pray for their "buddies."** During Sing & Play Stampede, Cowpoke Crafts and Missions, or Showtime Roundup, allow a short time for kids to pray for the children who will receive the Prayer Bears and books. Your children can pray that these children will discover how much Jesus loves each of us.

AFTER AVALANCHE RANCH

- **Send your Prayer Bears and Bible books to the Kid-to-Kid Send-Off Center.** Place the books and bears in a sturdy shipping box. Be sure to include $25 to help with ministry and distribution costs. Stuff the box with newspaper or newsprint to keep the books from shifting or possibly tearing. (Please send *only* the bears and books. Don't include other items or other stuffed animals.)

- **Look for your Operation Kid-to-Kid update.** International Bible Society will send your church a newsletter about Operation Kid-to-Kid several months after your program. You'll learn how this outreach program affected thousands of children around the world. Share this powerful information with your children; they'll love hearing that their gifts went around the world to share the message of Jesus' love! (We'll try to keep you posted on any distribution news at www.ok2k.org.)

Field Test Findings You may be used to holding "boys versus girls" contests to persuade kids to participate in missions projects. We would encourage you *not* to make these methods part of your Operation Kid-to-Kid, simply because they're unnecessary and detract from the purpose of missions. Instead, help kids discover the joy that comes from sharing with others. It has been our experience that kids participate wholeheartedly without any extrinsic rewards.

BEARING GIFTS OF LOVE!

Group's Avalanche Ranch is partnering with International Bible Society to provide soft, cuddly Prayer Bears and copies of *The Survivor's Bible* booklet for orphans in Africa. As part of our Avalanche Ranch VBS, our church will join this exciting missions project.

Kids will create bears that say "Jesus" in English, French, and Spanish. Every time recipients cuddle up with these bears, they'll be reminded of Jesus' love! Plus, kids will personalize special French versions of a booklet created for at-risk children, called *The Survivor's Bible*.

If you'd like to contribute to this exciting program, contact

_____
VBS Director

at _____ for more information.
Phone

OPERATION KID-TO-KID™
NEWS RELEASE

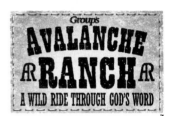

Adapt the information in this news release to fit your church's Avalanche Ranch. Then submit typed, double-spaced copies to your local newspapers, radio stations (especially your Christian radio station), and TV stations. You may want to check with them for any other specific requirements regarding news releases.

[Name of church] will be involved in a worldwide missions project called Operation Kid-to-Kid™. For this project, children attending [name of church]'s Avalanche Ranch vacation Bible school will provide soft Prayer Bears and copies of *The Survivor's Bible* for orphans in Africa.

Operation Kid-to-Kid will show kids that with Jesus' help, they can impact their world. The Prayer Bears will be shipped to International Bible Society, who will distribute them to orphans in Central and South Africa.

Because of children's generosity, Operation Kid-to-Kid has grown to become one of the world's largest global outreaches of children serving children.

Past Operation Kid-to-Kid programs have allowed more than a million children in North America to send hundreds of thousands of hygiene items, Spanish Bible materials, blankets, and shoes and socks to children around the world. (For more information about Operation Kid-to-Kid, visit www.ok2k.org.)

Operation Kid-to-Kid is just one part of Avalanche Ranch! Avalanche Ranch begins [starting date] and continues through [ending date]. It's located at [name of church and church address]. Registration opens each day at [starting time] and closes at [ending time]. For more information, call [church phone number].

Frequently Asked Questions

How do I sign up?
If you're participating in Group's Avalanche Ranch VBS, you're already "signed up"!

Do I have to buy the VBS Starter Kit to participate?
No. Even if you're not hosting an Avalanche Ranch VBS, you can get involved in Operation Kid-to-Kid. Making Prayer Bears is a great mission project for...
- Small groups
- Youth groups
- Women's groups
- Seniors' Bible studies
- Any group in your church that has a heart for missions

How many Prayer Bear kits will I need?
At Avalanche Ranch, we recommend purchasing two Prayer Bears per child. Each child will create one Prayer Bear to send to Africa and one Prayer Bear to keep. The Prayer Bear the child keeps serves as a reminder to pray for the children in Africa.

How long does it take to complete a Prayer Bear?
A child can complete two bears in less than an hour. Adult small groups may be able to work more quickly—it depends on how distracted they get while talking!

How do you make a Prayer Bear?
It's easy!
1. Open the Velcro closures on the bear.
2. Stuff the bear with small handfuls of Poly-Fil.
3. Close the Velcro closures.
4. Personalize and tuck the provided message (it's in the Daily Challenge strips) inside the bear. You'll even find a special sticker inside each Wild Ride Bible Guide. Add the sticker to the message card to share God's love in three different languages!

OPERATION KID-TO-KID

Where do I get Prayer Bears?

Prayer Bear kits are available from Group by calling 1-800-447-1070 or online at www.group.com/vbs. You can also order them from Group VBS suppliers.

Can I create Prayer Bears using my own pattern and materials?

Sure—but you'll find that the special mission price of this kit lets you get the polar fleece cheaper here than elsewhere. Plus it's pre-cut and has a handy pocket and Velcro closures already in place.

Also, if you plan to send your Prayer Bears to Africa through International Bible Society, they must be printed in English, French, and Spanish. It's important that items distributed among children are identical so no one feels left out.

Do I have to send the Prayer Bears to International Bible Society for distribution?

Feel free to tweak your OK2K program so you can use your bears as a local community service project—or send the items with your church mission team.

Can my preschoolers help?

Absolutely! Preschoolers love to stuff the bears with Poly-Fil. Little ones will be proud that they helped make these soft, cuddly bears!

What do I do with the bears when we're finished?

Once your Avalanche Ranch ends, send your completed Prayer Bears to International Bible Society for distribution. Here's how...

1. Look at each bear to be sure it's finished.

2. Place the bears and copies of *The Survivor's Bible* in a sturdy box. Please include a check for $25 made out to International Bible Society. This helps defray distribution costs.

3. Seal the box and mail it to:

> International Bible Society
> c/o Operation Kid-to-Kid
> 1820 Jet Stream Drive
> Colorado Springs, CO 80921

Planning Your Avalanche Ranch

Follow these steps to make your Avalanche Ranch the strongest VBS around!

PLANNING CALENDAR

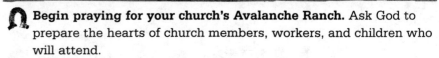

3 TO 6 MONTHS BEFORE AVALANCHE RANCH

Trail Tip

We frequently hear from customers who hold a very nontraditional VBS—using different settings, times, or dates. Be creative and choose the best VBS setting for your church situation. Avalanche Ranch is ultraflexible.

Begin praying for your church's Avalanche Ranch. Ask God to prepare the hearts of church members, workers, and children who will attend.

Choose a format for your Avalanche Ranch.

✔ Will you meet in the morning, afternoon, or evening?

✔ Will you meet every day for a week or once a week for several weeks?

✔ Will your program be for children only, or will entire families be invited to attend?

✔ Will you meet at your church or another location?

Set Avalanche Ranch dates. As you're considering dates, you may want to find out about other summer programs offered by your church or your community so you can avoid conflicts.

Choose a director. If you're reading this manual, that's you! The director is responsible for planning, recruiting staff, and overseeing all details to ensure that Avalanche Ranch flows smoothly. For an even easier adventure, consider recruiting a Crew Leader Director who will train, encourage, and check in on crew leaders throughout Avalanche Ranch. (Remember, your new favorite word is *delegate*!)

Field Test Findings

We've heard from many directors who have had terrific success with simple, creative fundraisers. (Some nearly doubled their budgets!) Remember, you're providing a high-quality children's ministry event. Don't be nervous about raising extra funds to make your program the best it can be. Ask these fundraising fans for advice on our message board at www.group.com/vbs!

Set a budget. Look through the entire Avalanche Ranch catalog to get an idea of what you'll need for your program. Write down the cost of each item you'll need, and then tally the total cost to set your budget. Your church may already include VBS in its budget. If so, find out what funds are available. If your church doesn't have a VBS budget in place, don't worry! *Money for a quality VBS program needn't be a stumbling block.* There are countless ways that you can easily (and painlessly) raise the funds you need. Consider the following ideas:

✔ Collect an offering to cover expenses.

✔ Charge a per-child registration fee for Avalanche Ranch. Give discounts to families that register more than one child.

✔ Invite congregation members to "sponsor" children by contributing a per-child amount. (See the "Registration" section on page 153 for more specifics on this idea.)

✔ Hold a creative fundraiser! Have a few staff members try their hand at making a batch of cowboy chili. Set out bowls and crackers, and ask for small donations for those who would like

PLANNING

to judge the chili contest. You might find a fantastic chef in addition to raising extra money for VBS!

Cindy's City Slicker Chili

Pastor Tom's Trailblazin' Chili

Caroline's Cowboy Chili

$1 per taste...
IF YOU DARE!

✔ Use the easy Fund-Your-VBS Kit (found in your Avalanche Ranch Starter Kit). With this simple kit, it's a snap to raise money, excitement, and awareness for your Avalanche Ranch. Simply slip the paper prairie dogs into church bulletins. Indicate how much each is worth—you set the price. When people turn in their prairie dogs and donations, tape the prairie dogs onto the giant poster (included in the kit), taped up in your children's ministry area. You'll be amazed at the funds that "pop up" for your VBS!

Start collecting decorations. Look for old cowboy boots, hats, ropes, bandannas, wheelbarrows, and buckets. You might even let members of your congregation know what you're looking for so they can keep their eyes and ears open for potential decorations. At our field test, we were able to borrow saddles and other real horse tack, a roping steer, and even a decorative wagon!

Come see www.groupoutlet.com. It's overflowing with the wildest decorations you've ever seen. Banners, bulletin board cutouts, T-shirts, and more are all at www.groupoutlet.com! You'll find decorating delights, clothing, Avalanche Ranch exclusives, and more resources at bargain prices.

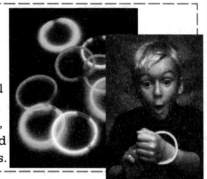

PLANNING

2 TO 3 MONTHS BEFORE AVALANCHE RANCH

Plan Avalanche Ranch publicity. Decide how you'll promote Avalanche Ranch in your church and community. Refer to the "Publicity" section (pp. 145-151) in this manual for publicity ideas and resources.

Set up your Avalanche Ranch church Web site. Go to www.group.com/vbs to access the VBS Web Toybox. Follow the easy steps to set up a Web site for your church's Avalanche Ranch. You can even choose to include your Avalanche Ranch in a directory so people in your community—or people visiting your area—can find *your* VBS!

Encourage preregistration. With your VBS Web Toybox, families can register online from the comfort and convenience of their homes. Once your Avalanche Ranch Web site is up, paste your

URL (that's the Web address at the top of the screen) into your publicity items. Families can access your site and register, and staff members can fill out staff applications. Plus, your Web Toybox instantly place kids into crews when they sign up!

Begin recruiting station leaders. Use the recruiting helps detailed in the "Recruiting" section (p. 97) to catch your Avalanche Ranch volunteers. The "Recruiting" section also includes bonus ideas that will captivate people's hearts and minds, while allowing you to flex those creative muscles (in an easy way—with great results). And the photocopiable job descriptions, handouts, and bulletin inserts make your job a breeze.

Estimate your Avalanche Ranch enrollment. Use figures from your church's Sunday school or figures from last year's VBS program. Once you've estimated how many children will attend, figure out how many Ranch Crew Leaders you'll need. You'll need one adult or teenage Ranch Crew Leader for every five children, including preschoolers. Be sure to have extra crew leaders ready in case you need to form Ranch Crews for last-minute registrants.

Order Avalanche Ranch materials. If you purchased the Avalanche Ranch Starter Kit, you already have a leader manual for every station and all the multimedia components you need. You may want to order additional leader manuals for team teaching— and a copy of each leader manual for yourself, if you'd like. We also recommend that you purchase the *Clip Art, Decorating, and Song Lyrics* CD, which includes customizable forms, decorating outlines, song lyrics, and more than 200 pieces of clip art.

For every elementary-age child, you'll *need* to order one of these items:

✔ Wild Ride Bible Guide (includes Daily Challenges and *The Survivor's Bible* for Operation Kid-to-Kid)

✔ Avalanche Ranch name badge

✔ set of Bible Memory Buddies

✔ Bible Point Craft items:
  - Buddy Bag
  - Prayer Journal or Shining Star Memorial
  - Operation Kid-to-Kid Prayer Bear (each child will make 2 bears)
  - Wild West Chalkboard or Boot Birdhouse
  - Cattle Drive Maze or Make-Your-Own Sheriff's Badge

For every preschooler, you'll *need* to order one of these items:

✔ Prairie Dog Bible Book (includes Daily Challenges and *The Survivor's Bible* for Operation Kid-to-Kid)

✔ Avalanche Ranch name badge

✔ set of Bible Memory Buddies

✔ Bible Point Craft items:
  - Buddy Bag
  - Prayer Journal
  - Operation Kid-to-Kid Prayer Bear (each child will make 2 bears)
  - Wild West Chalkboard
  - Make-Your-Own Sheriff's Badge

For every crew leader, you'll *need* to order one of these items:

- ✔ Avalanche Ranch name badge
- ✔ Preschool or Elementary Crew Leader Pocket Guide
- ✔ 1 set of Daily Challenge Wow Cows
- ✔ 1 Crew Bag

Even if you're planning a late-summer program, it's not too early to order materials. As you update your registration count, you can order additional student supplies as needed.

Explore your church facilities. You'll want to be deliberate in selecting your station areas. If your plans involve more than 150 children, run two or more simultaneous stations. For more information on how to do this, see "Ranch Stations" (p. 26). You'll need to set up a separate room or area for each station. Use the following guidelines:

- ✔ large room to accommodate entire VBS (possibly a sanctuary or fellowship hall)
- ✔ sound system/microphone (helpful)
- ✔ outlet to plug in CD player (or a sound system to play *Sing & Play Stampede Music* CD)
- ✔ outlet to plug in overhead projector (if using Sing & Play Stampede song lyrics transparencies)
- ✔ screen and video projection unit (for your music video)

- ✔ classroom to accommodate one-fourth of the elementary-age kids (helpful if room can be darkened)
- ✔ outlet to plug in TV and DVD player
- ✔ DVD player

- ✔ classroom to accommodate one-fourth of the elementary-age kids
- ✔ 1 or 2 low tables (helpful for supplies)
- ✔ outlet to plug in CD player when using *Sing & Play Stampede Music* CD

- ✔ large room to accommodate entire VBS (possibly a fellowship hall or gymnasium)
- ✔ church kitchen or other uncarpeted area for Chuck Wagon Chow Service

Important! As we've said, people who have used Group's VBS in the past tell us that their VBS programs are growing. To avoid stress and disappointment, **order early and order extra!**

Trail Tip Remember, kids *will* need ample space between their crews. In close quarters, kids will be bumping into other crews, making it nearly impossible for them to focus on the life-application discussions. A good guideline is to estimate that you'll need *at least* 3 feet of space between each crew. If your classrooms are small, divide into two smaller rooms so children can stretch out and have some privacy for discussion within their crews. It will make a *world* of difference!

Field Test Findings During Cowpoke Crafts and Missions, we found that it's easier for children to work on the floor rather than at tables. You may want to have a few chairs for crew leaders who need them.

Trail Tip You might have children pick up their snacks inside after praying together and learning the meaning of the snack. Then children can go directly outside to eat. You'll find this is less messy, gives children the opportunity to enjoy the sunshine, and provides a few crumbs for the birds!

✔ room or outdoor area to accommodate one-fourth of the elementary-age kids (a fellowship hall, gymnasium, or lawn)

✔ room enough for children to run around

✔ outlet to plug in CD player if using *Sing & Play Stampede Music* CD

✔ classroom that can comfortably accommodate one-fourth of the elementary-age kids and that can be darkened. Since the Wild Bible Adventures room requires "sets," it's helpful if this room can be undisturbed for the entire Avalanche Ranch.

✔ classroom that's in a quiet area of your facility (helpful for storytelling)

✔ outlet to plug in CD player

✔ large room to accommodate entire VBS (possibly a sanctuary or fellowship hall; could use the same room as Sing & Play Stampede)

✔ sound system/microphone (helpful)

✔ outlet to plug in CD player

✔ video projection unit

✔ large screen (for showing *Sing & Play Stampede Music* video and Spotlight Drama PowerPoint presentation)

✔ stage (helpful)

✔ up to 4 classroom(s) to accommodate all preschoolers for Crafts and Play, Games, Chadder's Theater, and Bible Adventures and Missions

✔ outlet to plug in TV/DVD player

✔ DVD player

✔ restroom facilities in room or nearby

✔ child-size furniture

✔ preschool toys such as blocks, modeling dough, dress-up clothes, and stuffed animals

Plan and schedule a leader training meeting using the guidelines in the "Staff Training Meeting" section (p. 128). This outline incorporates the *Wah-hoo! Recruiting, Overview, and Pass-Along Training* DVD, which contains clips from Avalanche Ranch field tests. Your station leaders will enjoy seeing Avalanche Ranch in action. Be sure to include Ranch Crew Leaders in your training so they can better understand their role. The DVD is filled with helpful, practical tips to make station leaders and crew leaders the best staff around. Plan to meet for at least two hours.

8 WEEKS BEFORE AVALANCHE RANCH

Begin recruiting Ranch Crew Leaders. Ranch Crew Leaders are like older brothers and sisters in the Ranch Crew family. They aren't responsible for teaching, and they don't have to prepare anything. Ranch Crew Leaders can be teenagers, college students, parents, or grandparents. They need only to love the Lord and love children. For more information on recruiting, see the "Recruiting" section beginning on page 97.

Ranch Crew Leaders should plan to participate in Avalanche Ranch for the entire adventure. If they need to be absent one or more days, encourage them to find their own substitutes.

Begin publicity. Fill in your program's dates and times on the Avalanche Ranch outdoor banner (available from Group Publishing and your Group supplier). Display the banner in a prominent outdoor location.

Hang Avalanche Ranch publicity posters (available from Group Publishing and your Group supplier) in your church and community.

Show the promotional segment of the *Wah-hoo!* DVD during a worship service or other church gathering. This brief segment gives people a glimpse of how Avalanche Ranch works and what kids will learn at this awesome VBS. You'll find that the video helps build enthusiasm, recruit volunteers, and promote attendance for your program. Be sure to follow up the video by telling the congregation how excited you are about the program!

Begin gathering supplies. Refer to the master supply list in the "Avalanche Ranch Daily Supplies" section (p. 76). (Note: Some stations may not require all the supplies listed, since station leaders can choose which activities they would like to do.) Consult with station leaders to inform them of how you'll handle supply collection. Will you gather all supplies, or will each leader gather his or her own supplies? You may want to ask church members to donate food supplies (such as pretzels and apples) or easy-to-find items (such as decorations).

Trail Tip: If you can't arrange for all your leaders to make it to the leader training meeting, consider videotaping the meeting. Send copies of the videotape to volunteers who couldn't make it. If you can't videotape the session, send the *Wah-hoo!* DVD to your leaders to help them better prepare for their roles.

Trail Tip: Ranch Crew Leaders play such an important role at your VBS. They form important relationships with kids, take part in life-application discussions, and will get to know kids better than anyone else involved in your program. Prepare them for this task with the Crew Leader Pocket Guide. This simple handbook is filled with easy, practical tips that will make your Ranch Crew Leaders the best! Plus, it includes discussion questions from Wild Bible Adventures, Chadder's Wild West Theater, and Horseplay Games. (Available for both preschool and elementary crew leaders, Crew Leader Pocket Guides are available from Group Publishing or your Group supplier.)

PLANNING

Trail Tip Trimming time from your Avalanche Ranch doesn't have to be a challenge. You can shave a few minutes from Sing & Play Stampede and Showtime Roundup by simply reducing the number of songs kids sing. (But don't cut the singing completely!) Cut back on travel time between stations, as well as the time needed for kids to eat snacks. *Please don't cut out important things like Chadder's Wild West Theater (where kids make important life-application Bible connections) or Operation Kid-to-Kid (which allows kids to share God's love in a tangible way). Each element of this program is there for a reason. Cutting out these elements is like throwing away pieces of a puzzle.*

Trail Tip If you're planning to offer a nursery program or child care for staff, be sure to check out the Little Buckaroos Infants, Toddlers, and Twos program. Even the littlest learners will love learning about God's love!

Plan your Avalanche Ranch schedule. The average VBS program runs for up to three hours each day. Group's Avalanche Ranch materials have been developed with these parameters in mind. For a three-hour program, Sing & Play Stampede and Showtime Roundup should last 25 minutes each, and every other station should last 20 minutes. See the daily schedules on pages 85-86 to see how this works. If your program will meet for more or less time than three hours each day, you'll need to adapt these times accordingly.

You can find customizable Daily Schedules on your VBS Web Toybox, too!

4 WEEKS BEFORE AVALANCHE RANCH

Recruit additional volunteers. In addition to station leaders and Ranch Crew Leaders, you may want to recruit volunteers to help with registration, transportation, and child care for the staff. Refer to the "Recruiting" section for more ideas.

Get your congregation excited about Operation Kid-to-Kid. Check out the Operation Kid-to-Kid section of this manual (p. 45) to find easy ways to get everyone involved with this missions project.

Continue publicity. Mail Avalanche Ranch invitation postcards to children in your church and community. Distribute Avalanche Ranch doorknob danglers in your community. Write your church's name and when your Avalanche Ranch will begin. (Invitation postcards and doorknob danglers are available from Group Publishing or your Group supplier.) Be sure to direct people to your Avalanche Ranch Web site for easy registration.

Continue preregistration. Photocopy the "Avalanche Ranch Registration Form" (p. 172). Insert copies in your church bulletins, distribute copies in Sunday school classes, and keep a supply in your church office. Encourage parents from your church to preregister their children and their children's friends. (Remember, when families register online, they'll automatically be put into crews, making your job even easier.) This will make your first day more manageable.

Hold the scheduled leader training meeting. Plan to meet in a large room where you'll be able to try out some Avalanche Ranch snacks and activities. Before the meeting, set up a TV and DVD player, and decorate the room using the suggestions provided in the staff training outline (p. 128). Bring the station leader manuals, Crew Leader Pocket Guides, and photocopies of the "For Ranch Crew Leaders Only" handouts (pp. 139-142).

Meet with each station leader. It's a good idea to touch base with each station leader on a one-on-one basis. Take each person to lunch or out for ice cream, or simply go for a walk together as you discuss what supplies the leader needs, what concerns he or she may have, or any aspects of the program that are not clear. This will not only prevent miscommunication but also help your volunteers know how much you appreciate them.

Trail Tip
Preregistration really does make things run more smoothly. To get more kids preregistered, you might offer incentives. For example, provide an Avalanche Ranch T-shirt or a *Sing & Play Stampede Music* audiocassette for each child who registers early. Or fill a large jar with Jolly Ranchers candy. Children who preregister can submit a "guess" as to how many candies are in the jar. (The winner gets to keep the entire jar of candy! Yum!) These incentives will build enthusiasm for your VBS, too.

IMPORTANT TRAINING INFO

Although station leaders may want to add their flair or creativity to an activity, drama, or craft, encourage them to stick as closely as possible to the written material. Remind your staff members that each element of the Avalanche Ranch program has been designed (and tested) to fit with the others—sort of like a jigsaw puzzle. Remember, we want to make VBS easy for your staff. There's no need to re-create or reinvent the wheel!

Provide Avalanche Ranch information to your church office. Fill in your church's information on the community flier on page 150, and photocopy a stack of completed fliers on brightly colored paper to put in your church office. Someone in the office can refer to the fliers if people call with questions about your program and can distribute fliers to people who stop by the office.

If your church has a phone answering machine, you may also want to include Avalanche Ranch information in your recorded message. If your church has its own Web site, be sure to add Avalanche Ranch information there, too.

Start building your Daily Challenge Corral. The Daily Challenge is an *important* part of Avalanche Ranch. You'll need a place for crews to add their Daily Challenge Wow Cows each day. Not only is this a super, visual way to show that kids are living out the Bible Point, but it also becomes a focal point of your Sing & Play Stampede decorations. Use the directions on page 18, and work with the Sing & Play Stampede Leader to create a sturdy corral.

2 WEEKS BEFORE AVALANCHE RANCH

Trail Tip

It's a good idea to line up a few extra Ranch Crew Leaders who will be available in case you have lots of walk-in registrants. Remember, kids *and* leaders will have greater success if crews don't get larger than five kids. Be sure these Ranch Crew Leaders arrive early on Day 1 so they can step in if necessary. (Because no preparation is needed for Ranch Crew Leaders, it's easy for people to step in at any point.)

Check your registration count. Visit your Web Toybox home page for an instant registration count. Make sure you have enough student books for each child to have one. Order extras just in case; many churches experience last-minute additions, first-day surprises, and unexpected increases as kids bring their friends throughout the week. Also double-check that you have enough Ranch Crew Leaders, assigning one crew leader to five children.

Check your supply collection. Make a final announcement, or put a final supply list in your church bulletin. Gather or purchase additional supplies as necessary.

Continue publicity. Photocopy and fill out the news release (p. 149), and send copies to your local newspapers, radio stations, and TV stations. Use the snazzy clip art found on the *Clip Art, Song Lyrics, and Decorating* CD to create fliers, bulletins, posters, and more. This CD works with both Macintosh and PC-compatible computers.

Announce Avalanche Ranch in worship services and other church gatherings. Put bulletin inserts in your church's worship bulletins. (Bulletin inserts are available from Group Publishing or your local Group supplier.)

Before your worship service, have a few volunteers perform the publicity skit on page 151. Show the promotional segment of the *Wah-hoo!* DVD again.

Mail additional Avalanche Ranch invitation postcards as necessary.

Make backup and emergency plans. What if it rains during your program? Plan in advance how you'll handle bad weather. You may also want to line up backup Ranch Crew Leaders in case some drop out.

Inform station leaders and Ranch Crew Leaders of procedures to follow if there's a fire or other emergency.

1 WEEK BEFORE AVALANCHE RANCH

Dedicate Avalanche Ranch staff. Introduce station leaders, Ranch Crew Leaders, and other volunteers during your church service. Then have your pastor or other church members pray that God will use these workers to touch kids' lives with his love during Avalanche Ranch.

Assign kids to Ranch Crews. If you're using your Web Toybox, this step is automatically done for you! If not, photocopy the "Ranch Crew Roster" (p. 169). You'll need one roster for each

PLANNING

crew. Using the preregistration forms you've received, assign children to elementary and preschool Ranch Crews. Each Ranch Crew should have no more than five children and one adult or teenage Ranch Crew Leader. Be sure that each preschool Ranch Crew has a mix of 3-, 4-, and 5-year-olds.

Here are some additional guidelines for assigning crews:

✔ Fill in the "Ranch Crew Roster" (p. 169) in pencil—you'll probably make changes as you work.

✔ Whenever possible, place a child from each age level in each Ranch Crew. If the age distribution at your program is uneven, include as wide an age range as you can. Guarantee success for everyone involved by *not* forming single-age Ranch Crews.

✔ Include a good mix of boys and girls in each Ranch Crew.

✔ If a child is bringing a friend, assign the two children to the same Ranch Crew if possible. If a child is bringing several friends, assign pairs of kids to different Ranch Crews.

✔ In general, it works best to assign siblings to different Ranch Crews. However, you know the children in your church. Use your judgment as to whether siblings should be together.

✔ If you anticipate behavior problems with certain children or have children with special needs, assign them to Ranch Crews that have more experienced adult Ranch Crew Leaders.

✔ If you have children who are particularly helpful or cooperative, assign them to Ranch Crews that have teenage Ranch Crew Leaders.

✔ If you want your program to have a strong outreach emphasis, limit each Ranch Crew to three children. Then encourage kids to fill their crews by bringing their friends.

✔ Remember to leave open spaces in a few crews for kids who haven't preregistered. *Your goal is to make sure each crew contains only five children.*

✔ After you've assigned elementary children to Ranch Crews, assign each crew to one of four larger groups. (Remember, one-fourth of the kids at VBS travel together at a time.) Label these four groups A, B, C, and D—or use your creativity to name them something that fits the Avalanche Ranch theme, such as buckaroos, wranglers, or trailblazers. Ranch Crews travel with their larger groups as they visit the stations each day. For more information about assigning Ranch Crews to groups, see page 83.

✔ Once you've finished assigning crews, double-check that you haven't forgotten anyone or double-booked anyone.

We've received count-less letters from Group VBS customers who have admitted they were skeptical about forming combined-age crews. But when these customers took a leap of faith and tried combined-age crews, they were amazed at how well they worked. Most people noted a decline in discipline problems, an increase in cooperation, and a special bonding among crew members.

If you're planning for a family VBS, assign entire families to each Ranch Crew. Then add single adults, grandparents, visiting children, or smaller families to the crews. Remember to leave several Ranch Crews open so that you can add new members on opening day.

Meet with station leaders again. Check with leaders to make sure they have all the required supplies, and answer any questions they may have. Work together to smooth out any last-minute details.

Decide when and where station leaders and Ranch Crew Leaders will meet each day. It's a good idea to have your staff arrive early on Day 1 to greet children and assist with registration. Be sure each Ranch Crew Leader has a large sign with his or her crew number or crew name written on it.

Help station leaders decorate their rooms. Use the decorating ideas found in the colorful VBS catalog, leader manuals, or the decorating booklet found in your Starter Kit to turn your church into a high mountain ranch. (Be sure to check out www.groupoutlet.com for the hottest decorations around...at bargain prices!)

DURING AVALANCHE RANCH

Meet with Ranch Crew Leaders during Sing & Play Stampede. Each day the Sing & Play Stampede Leader will excuse Ranch Crew Leaders for a quick huddle and prayer with you outside the Sing & Play Stampede area. This is a great time to ask crew leaders if they have any needs or concerns, to make last-minute announcements or schedule changes, and to encourage your crew leaders. Lead a prayer, asking God to bless your day, protect everyone, and give all leaders wisdom as they work with each child.

Register new children. Make sure you have plenty of workers on hand to register kids the first day. (This is an excellent way to use volunteers who aren't available to help the entire week.) Set up separate registration sites for preregistration check-in and walk-in registration. Follow the Day 1 registration procedures outlined on pages 161-164.

After Day 1, maintain a registration table to register kids who join your program midweek.

Meet with station leaders and Ranch Crew Leaders after each day's program. Check in with all Avalanche Ranch staff to see what went smoothly and what could be improved for future days. Be prepared to change schedules, rooms, or procedures. You may even need to reassign some Ranch Crews. Work together to make any necessary changes to ensure that everything runs smoothly.

Give announcements during Sing & Play Stampede or Showtime Roundup. During the course of the program, you may need to change schedules, stations, or Ranch Crew assignments.

You also may have personal messages or lost-and-found items to deliver to participants. Each day check with the Sing & Play Stampede Leader and Showtime Roundup Leader to schedule any announcements you would like everyone to hear.

Attend Sing & Play Stampede and Showtime Roundup each day. These opening and closing activities will give you a good indication of how your adventure is proceeding. They also provide opportunities for children to see you and to identify you as the director. Each day the Sing & Play Stampede Leader may call on you to pray before dismissing kids to their stations. Besides, you'll have fun!

Peek into as many stations as you can. We visit a variety of VBS programs every year, and we're amazed at how many directors don't really know what's happening in the classrooms. While you don't need to hover over the kids or make your station leaders nervous, it's important to know that leaders are following your guidelines.

Help your staff be the best it can be. Your helpful presence will let staff members know that they're not alone. Plus, you can make sure they're following the program so it will be powerful. Remember, station leaders need to follow the leader guides because each station plays an important role in children's overall learning experience.

Make sure all station leaders and Ranch Crew Leaders are present each day. Arrange for substitutes if necessary. If you're in a pinch for Ranch Crew Leaders, ask the Sing & Play Stampede Leader and Showtime Roundup Leader to fill in—or appoint yourself crew leader for a day.

Make sure station leaders and Ranch Crew Leaders have the supplies they need each day. Have a runner available to collect or purchase additional supplies if necessary.

Help with discipline problems as necessary. In Avalanche Ranch field tests (and from real programs across North America), workers encountered virtually no discipline problems. Each day was so full of fun Bible-learning activities that kids didn't have time to misbehave. Combined-age Ranch Crews encourage kids to work together instead of squabble, and minor problems can be handled by station leaders or Ranch Crew Leaders. So your job is easy!

Stock and maintain a first-aid site. Keep a good supply of adhesive bandages and first-aid ointment on hand along with phone numbers for local clinics and hospitals. You may also want to keep photocopies of kids' registration forms near your first-aid site. You can use the forms to check for allergies or other health concerns. Be sure to tell your Ranch Crew Leaders of any allergies or special needs, too.

Field Test Findings

During our field test, our staff and crew leaders met each afternoon for prayer and lunch and to talk about the highlights of the day. This was a fun time for volunteers to relax and share stories about what had happened at their stations or about what the kids in their Ranch Crews had done. Not only did we glean important information (to include in the finished program), but it also gave everyone a peek at the other fun things going on at Avalanche Ranch.

Field Test Findings

One day our team peeked into a local VBS, only to discover that one station leader was working on the wrong day's Bible Point. Whoops!

Trail Tip

It's important to check your registration forms for any mention of food allergies. Let the Chuck Wagon Chow Leader know as soon as possible so that he or she can make alternative snacks if necessary.

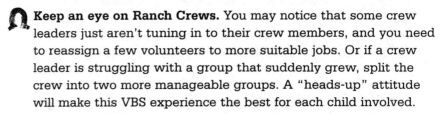

Keep an eye on Ranch Crews. You may notice that some crew leaders just aren't tuning in to their crew members, and you need to reassign a few volunteers to more suitable jobs. Or if a crew leader is struggling with a group that suddenly grew, split the crew into two more manageable groups. A "heads-up" attitude will make this VBS experience the best for each child involved.

Prepare Avalanche Ranch completion certificates. Photocopy and fill out a certificate for each child. An Avalanche Ranch completion certificate is in the Starter Kit, and additional certificates are available from Group Publishing and your Group supplier.

Send the memories home! We've heard it again and again: "My kids can't stop singing those songs!" Plan to provide (or sell) *Sing & Play Stampede Music* audiocassettes or CDs for the kids at your program. Set up a table, complete with information on how to obtain Sing & Play Stampede media items, outside your Showtime Roundup area. Check out the reduced prices in the VBS catalog. (One church we visited already had them available at the registration table on the first day.) There's even a bonus poster in your Fund-Your-VBS Kit to help sell these awesome family resources.

AFTER AVALANCHE RANCH

Collect reusable leftover supplies. Store the supplies in your church's supply closet or resource room for use in future VBS programs or other children's ministry events. If you borrowed supplies such as pool noodles, buckets, or cassette players, return them to their owners.

Send your Operation Kid-to-Kid Prayer Bears and *The Survivor's Bible* books to International Bible Society. (For more information, see the "Operation Kid-to-Kid" section beginning on page 45 or visit www.ok2k.org.) The Showtime Roundup Leader may have these from the Day 5 program.

Leave rooms decorated for your next church service. If outreach was an emphasis during Avalanche Ranch, you'll be pleased when visitors from your VBS program come for church. They'll feel more comfortable returning to a familiar environment. Also, church members will enjoy getting a glimpse of Avalanche Ranch.

Follow up with Avalanche Ranch visitors. Mail Avalanche Ranch follow-up postcards or mailable Foto Frames (available from Group Publishing and your Group supplier). Encourage Ranch Crew Leaders to make personal contact with the members of their Ranch Crews within two weeks after VBS. Use the additional follow-up ideas beginning on page 189 in this manual.

Report on your program. During your next worship service, invite station leaders, Ranch Crew Leaders, and kids who attended Avalanche Ranch to share their favorite VBS experiences. Encourage kids to display their Bible Point Crafts. You may even want to invite the Sing & Play Stampede Leader to lead everyone in singing one or two favorite Avalanche Ranch songs. When others see how much fun VBS can be, your recruiting will be a breeze next year! In fact, they may even sign up for *next year's* VBS on the spot!

Present a slide show or video, or post photos from your program. Just show all the Spotlight Drama presentations back-to-back. (The work is already done!) Kids (and their parents) love seeing themselves on the "big screen." And colorful photos will bring back memories of a terrific time at Avalanche Ranch.

Meet with your entire Avalanche Ranch staff to evaluate your program. Celebrate the best VBS ever! Make written notes of good ideas that could be used for next year's program. Note any problems that came up and how they were solved. Brainstorm about ways to avoid similar problems in the future. Include notes of how you adapted the Avalanche Ranch materials to fit your church. Record the names of Ranch Crew Leaders and station leaders who are interested in helping again next year. Post the "Join the Team!" handout (p. 194), and allow interested volunteers to sign up for next year's program. (You'll be surprised at the number who will!) Bring the Avalanche Ranch evaluation forms included in this manual (pp. 196-197), and have staff members fill them out.

Thank your staff members for all their hard work. Use the Howdy plush toy to thank and affirm your volunteers. Attach a note that says, "Thanks for digging into Horseplay Games" or "You were top (prairie) dog in Chuckwagon Chow." Howdy plush toys are available from Group Publishing and your Group supplier. You could even hand out balloons, flowers, or baked goodies to show your appreciation. For more thematic ideas, see page 193.

Fill out the "Avalanche Ranch Evaluation." Fill out the online VBS director's evaluation at www.group.com/vbs. This helps us plan for the future.

Thanks for digging into Horseplay Games!

WHEN AND WHERE TO HAVE VBS

If your church has put on VBS programs before, you probably have a good idea of the times and settings that work best in your situation. Use the suggested times and settings listed below to spark creativity as you plan your Avalanche Ranch!

OPTIONS FOR AVALANCHE RANCH LOCATIONS

Your church: Many VBS programs are held in local churches. With this approach, you control the facilities, you have many rooms available, and the station is familiar to church members. Plus, visitors who come to Avalanche Ranch actually visit your church site. (If your church facility isn't large enough, consider teaming up with another local church that might have more room. You'll double your resources and have twice the impact, while showing kids that God's family can do great things when we work together!)

> Don't get stuck in a boring routine! Avalanche Ranch is so flexible! You can choose the program that's best for your church.

A local park: Kids love being outdoors, and parks draw children who would not normally attend a VBS program. Check with your local parks and recreation department to see about reserving a park or campground for your Avalanche Ranch. Church, YMCA, and scout camps provide ideal outdoor settings since they usually have electricity available. Consider renting a large tent or canopy to use in your outdoor setting.

Inner city: Turn your Avalanche Ranch program into an inner city outreach opportunity. Invite kids from your church to join inner city kids in an inner city church or neighborhood setting. Even if you use only portions of the Avalanche Ranch materials, you'll help needy children and their families understand Jesus' love.

A local school: Since most schools lie dormant for the majority of the summer, consider using their facilities for your program. If public schools are busy with summer classes, check out Christian school facilities in your area.

A backyard or home: Backyard Bible clubs are a wonderful way to build relationships and a sense of community in your neighborhood. Sing & Play Stampede and Showtime Roundup can take place in the backyard, while other stations rotate through the dining room, living room, or basement. With a little creativity, you can welcome a small number of children into your home to hear the good news of God's love!

OPTIONS FOR AVALANCHE RANCH TIMES

Weekday mornings: Many programs are held for five consecutive weekday mornings. Kids have plenty of energy, and the summer sun isn't quite as hot as in the afternoon. For a change of pace, you could even plan to hold a morning program during your students' spring break.

Weekday afternoons: Afternoons may be a new option for many churches, but we've heard from directors who say it's the best. Preschoolers have had naps, older kids are done with morning soccer practice, and everyone is ready for fun!

Weekday evenings: Since many church members work during the day, some churches find it easier to staff an evening program. This could be a special program that you hold for five consecutive evenings, or it could take the place of an existing midweek program. If you hold your Avalanche Ranch program in the evening, you may want to include families. You can offer separate programming for parents and teenagers or include them in Avalanche Ranch as full-fledged participants and Ranch Crew Leaders. Church members of all ages will enjoy visiting the stations. Each family can form its own Ranch Crew, or you can mix families and enlist parents as Ranch Crew Leaders. If you invite families, you'll want to provide child care for children younger than 3 years old.

Midweek clubs: If your church has a midweek club or another weekly children's program, you may want to use the Avalanche Ranch materials for five consecutive weeks. If you use Avalanche Ranch during a regularly scheduled midweek program, you'll probably have station leaders already in place. Just assign Ranch Crews and recruit Ranch Crew Leaders, and you'll be ready to start the adventure!

Day camp: Extend Avalanche Ranch to a half-day day camp for kids in your community. (Again, consider holding your day camp during spring break.) We've provided extra crafts, plenty of games, and lots of upbeat songs to keep children actively learning Bible truths...and having a great time!

Sunday mornings: Hold Avalanche Ranch during your normal Sunday school or children's church time. This is a great change of pace for summer for both kids and children's workers. (Plus, it's a wonderful way for families to participate.)

Weekend retreat: Invite children or whole families to participate in a weekend retreat held at your church or a local camp. Schedule Day 1 activities for Saturday morning, Days 2 and 3 for Saturday afternoon (after lunch), Day 4 for Saturday evening (after dinner), and Day 5 for Sunday morning.

PLANNING

Ten-day VBS: Some churches like to do a full two-week program. There's plenty of material in your Avalanche Ranch leader manuals to do just that. You'll cover each Bible story and Point two days in a row. The first day, kids will go to Wild Bible Adventures but not Chadder's Wild West Theater. On the second day, kids won't have Wild Bible Adventures, but they *will* attend Chadder's Wild West Theater. The other manuals contain loads of extra games, songs, and bonus crafts that will allow you to use the same Bible Point and story two days in a row. And kids will have an even easier time remembering these awesome, life-changing Bible truths.

FOR A SUPER EVENING PROGRAM...

The following tips will help your evening or intergenerational program go smoothly:

Start early so young children won't get too tired.

Consider beginning each session with a simple meal. Recruit a kitchen team to organize potlucks or prepare simple meals such as hot dogs or frozen pizzas. If your church has a lawn or grassy area nearby, you may even want to barbecue. Families will enjoy this casual interaction time, and you'll be able to start your program earlier.

Make sure children who attend without their families have safe transportation to and from Avalanche Ranch. Don't allow children to walk home alone in the dark, even if they live nearby.

Families come in all shapes and sizes. Be sensitive to single-parent families, childless couples, and children who come alone. You may want to assign family members to separate Ranch Crews to avoid drawing attention to family differences.

Be creative as you plan for Avalanche Ranch!

AVALANCHE RANCH DAILY SUPPLIES

Station	Supplies You'll Use Every Day	Day 1	Day 2
Sing & Play Stampede	Bible, *Sing & Play Stampede Music Leader Version* CD*, Avalanche Ranch name badge*, cassette or CD player, photocopies of the "Who's Who on the Crew?" handout, Bible Point posters*, microphone/sound system, Wrangler Ringer* or other attention-getting signal, lyrics transparencies printed from the *Clip Art, Song Lyrics, and Decorating* CD* (optional), overhead projector (optional), props for Avalanche Ranch skits (optional), Daily Challenge Wow Cows*	props for Avalanche Ranch skits (optional)	props for Avalanche Ranch skits (optional)
Cowpoke Crafts and Missions	supplies for Bible Point Crafts* (see the options given each day), Bible Point posters* (optional), *Sing & Play Stampede Music* audiocassette or CD* (optional), cassette or CD player (optional), Wrangler Ringer* or other attention-getting device, wristwatch or clock	**Buddy Bag**—1 Buddy Bag* per child, one 36-inch length of yarn per child, six 8-inch lengths of yarn per child, variety of beads, Glue Dots** (optional), "Wrap-Up Questions" handout, finished sample of a Buddy Bag, 1 complete set of Bible Memory Buddies*, Operation Kid-to-Kid poster pack*, TV and DVD player, *Wah-hoo!* DVD*	**Prayer Journal**—1 Prayer Journal Kit* per child (a Prayer Journal Kit contains 1 cover, 1 cord, 1 notepad, and 1 star button), colorful permanent markers, glue sticks, Bible Memory Buddy Stampers* (optional), "Wrap-Up Questions" handout, finished sample of a Prayer Journal, Operation Kid-to-Kid poster of Ibrahim and Adamou* **Shining Star Memorial**—1 Shining Star Memorial Kit* per child (a Shining Star Memorial Kit contains 1 sheet of sturdy embossing foil, 1 pattern, 1 lanyard, and 4 framing sticks), Glue Dots** (4 per child), ballpoint pens (1 per child), 1 old magazine per child (for kids to press on as they draw), markers, double-sided tape, "Wrap-Up Questions" handout, Operation Kid-to-Kid poster of Ibrahim and Adamou*, finished sample of a Shining Star Memorial
Horseplay Games	Wrangler Ringer* or other attention-getter, *Sing & Play Stampede Music* CD* (optional), CD player (optional), sample Crew Leader Pocket Guide*	**Truth Talks**—none **Spy Sneak**—several pool noodles to mark boundaries **One and Only**—1 chair per participant	**Calf and Cattle Dog**—several pool noodles to mark boundaries **Jordan Memorial**—several pool noodles to mark boundaries, 1 sponge ball per participant, 1 bucket of water per crew, 1 spray bottle filled with water per crew **Shadows**—none

*These items are available from Group Publishing and your local Group supplier.

**available at www.groupoutlet.com

Many VBS directors requested a daily supply list so they could see what days certain supplies are needed. Check out the chart below to see if there are supplies that can be shared between stations. Chuck Wagon Chow is not included in the chart, due to the specific nature of the food items. (See page 80 for Chuck Wagon Chow supplies.) Also, check with the preschool director to see what supplies he or she will need each day. Be sure to look at supply lists in each station leader manual for more detail about supplies needed.

Day 3	Day 4	Day 5
props for Avalanche Ranch skits (optional)	props for Avalanche Ranch skits (optional)	props for Avalanche Ranch skits (optional)

Operation Kid-to-Kid Prayer Bears—2 Operation Kid-to-Kid Prayer Bears* per child, 1 bag of Poly-Fil, markers, "Wrap-Up Questions" handout, 2 finished Operation Kid-to-Kid Prayer Bears*, sample Wild Ride Bible Guide and *The Survivor's Bible*, Operation Kid-to-Kid poster of Khadim*, stuffed animal from home

Boot Birdhouse—1 Boot Birdhouse Kit* per child (each Boot Birdhouse Kit includes 5 birdhouse pieces and 1 cord), watercolor markers, rubber bands (1 per child), glue sticks, "Wrap-Up Questions" handout, finished sample of a Boot Birdhouse, Operation Kid-to-Kid poster of Mirielle*

Wild West Chalkboard—1 Wild West Chalkboard Kit* per child (each Wild West Chalkboard Kit contains 1 chalkboard, 5 custom foam shapes, 1 rope handle, and 1 Avalanche Ranch set of chalk), glue, markers (for writing names on craft projects), "Wrap-Up Questions" handout, completed Wild West Chalkboard, cotton ball or tissue, Operation Kid-to-Kid poster of Mirielle*

Cattle Drive Maze—1 Cattle Drive Maze Kit* per child (each Cattle Drive Maze Kit contains 1 base sheet, 3 custom metal steer shapes, 1 custom foam shape, 1 magnetic wand, and 1 plastic cover), glue sticks, markers, double-sided tape, "Wrap-Up Questions" handout, completed Cattle Drive Maze

Make-Your-Own Sheriff's Badge—1 Make-Your-Own Sheriff's Badge per child, pencils, 1 sheet of paper per child, double-sided tape, "Wrap-Up Questions" handout, completed Make-Your-Own Sheriff's Badge

No Smiling!—none

Empty the Pail—1 bucket of water per crew, 5 sponge balls per crew

Safe in the Corral—several pool noodles to make 2 corrals

Watering-Hole Relay—2 buckets per crew (1 filled with water), 1 pingpong ball per crew, masking tape

Ice Tag—several pool noodles to mark boundaries, at least 1 ice cube per participant, 1 cooler to keep ice frozen

This Is a Change-Up—none

Seven Showers—1 empty 1-gallon milk jug per crew, 1 wide plastic tub of water per crew, scissors

Who's the Boss?—3 types of attention-getters, such as the Wrangler Ringer*, a whistle, and a kazoo

Follow the Line—1 pingpong ball per crew, masking tape

PLANNING

Station	Supplies You'll Use Every Day	Day 1	Day 2
Wild Bible Adventures	Bible-times robe for you, stool, *Wild Bible Adventures Drama* CD*, CD player with "repeat" function, Wrangler Ringer*, blue sheets (1 per crew—reuse each rotation), four 6-foot stepladders, plastic plants (up to a dozen), dropcloths and lighting)	2 dowels or 3-foot sticks, red cord	spray bottle filled with water; flat river rocks about the size of a fist (enough for ¼ of the kids); small, dark, plastic tarp; safety pins; clothesline; pocketknife to cut clothesline; several dark towels
Chadder's Wild West Theater	Bible, *Chadder's Wild West Adventure* DVD*, TV and DVD player, 1 Wild Ride Bible Guide* per child, 1 Wild Ride Bible Guide from the Starter Kit* (for your example), 1 Bible Memory Buddies set* per child, newsprint and marker, 1 fine-tip marker or ballpoint pen per child, clock or watch with a second hand, Wrangler Ringer* or other attention-getting device, *Sing & Play Stampede Music* CD*, CD player, Treasure Verse posters* (optional)	1 dollar bill (1 per crew, for one-fourth of the total number of crews)	Stone Stickers* from the Wild Ride Bible Guide sticker sheets; 1 small bottle of vanilla-scented oil per crew (found at most craft and hobby stores); 1 flashlight per crew, plus 1 for the leader; white or light-colored wall
Showtime Roundup	Bible, CD player or sound system, *Sing & Play Stampede Music Leader Version* CD*, Wrangler Ringer* or other attention-getting signal, Bible Point posters*	Buc's Bible Point poster* and a rope (the Sing & Play Stampede Leader should have these), 1 extension cord, 1 large flashlight, 1 large fan, 1 table, 3 bright-colored bedsheets or tablecloths, Day 1 Daily Challenge (from a Wild Ride Bible Guide)	Shadow's Bible Point poster* and a bedsheet (the Sing & Play Stampede Leader should have these), blue paper, Day 2 Daily Challenge (from a Wild Ride Bible Guide)

*These items are available from Group Publishing and your local Group supplier.

**available at www.groupoutlet.com

PLANNING

Day 3	Day 4	Day 5
adult volunteer to play the role of Sergeant, Bible-times robe for the Sergeant, red cord from Day 1, plastic sword for the Sergeant	black armbands (1 per participant—reuse each rotation), glow bracelets** (1 per participant), 15 colorful helium balloons on strings, 15 river rocks from Day 2 to use as balloon anchors, electric campfire	room freshener (we used Febreze); fresh, quartered onions (1 per small group); 1 large pot of cold water per group (reuse each rotation); 1 stainless steel tablespoon per group (reuse each rotation); paper towels (10 sheets per group); unscented baby wipes; clipboard; 1-gallon resealable plastic bags; snack-sized resealable plastic bags; vanilla-scented oil (the Chadder's Wild West Theater Leader will use this on Day 1, so check to see if there are any leftovers); medical or drywall mask
1 hair dryer, 1 pingpong ball, 1 Chirping Chick**	Crayola Erasable markers**	1 small paper cup per child, pitchers, water, unsweetened lemonade mix, large spoon for stirring
Ranger's Bible Point poster* and 2 smaller boxes (the Sing & Play Stampede Leader should have these), Day 3 Daily Challenge (from a Wild Ride Bible Guide), 6 large boxes, clear fishing line, 4x6 cards elementary crews prepared during Wild Bible Adventures and preschoolers prepared during Chadder's Wild West Theater, Glue Dots**	Skye's Bible Point poster* and a small cross (the Sing & Play Stampede Leader should have these), Day 4 Daily Challenge (from a Wild Ride Bible Guide), 1 large cross, strings of Christmas lights—1 bulb per participant (the lights that have the individual circuits, not the continuous one), 1 staple gun, 1 resealable plastic bag per crew	Bible Point posters* and props from all 5 days—rope, bedsheet, boxes, small cross, and toy sword (the Sing & Play Stampede Leader should have these); Day 5 Daily Challenge (from a Wild Ride Bible Guide); 1 Daily Challenge Wow Cow* per crew; 1 table; 1 bright-colored tablecloth; 1 package of bright-colored sticky dots; 1 robe

HUCK WAGON CHOW

...icipants you're expecting (including children and crew leaders).
...amount" by the "total number of participants" to find out how much

		Required Amount	Total Number of Participants	Total Required Amount
DAY 1	frosted wheat cereal ✓	¼ cup per participant	X _____	= _____
	M&M's candies ✓	¼ cup per participant	X _____	= _____
	twisted pretzels ✓	¼ cup per participant	X _____	= _____
	red licorice bits ✓	¼ cup per participant	X _____	= _____
	raisins ✓	¼ cup per participant	X _____	= _____
	water or juice	1 quart for every 5 participants	X _____	= _____
DAY 2	graham crackers ✓	1 per participant	X _____	= _____
	chocolate candy bar ✓	½ bar per participant	X _____	= _____
	vanilla frosting ✓	about 2 tablespoons per participant	X _____	= _____
	water or juice	1 quart for every 5 participants	X _____	= _____
DAY 3	round crackers ✓	6 per participant	X _____	= _____
	pepperoni slices ✓	3 per partcipant	X _____	= _____
	cheese squares ✓	3 per participant	X _____	= _____
	water or juice	1 quart for every 5 participants	X _____	= _____
DAY 4	pre-packaged cups of vanilla ice cream ✓	1 per participant	X _____	= _____
	chocolate cookies ✓	1 per participant	X _____	= _____
	cherries ✓	1 per participant	X _____	= _____
	water or juice	1 quart for every 5 participants	X _____	= _____
DAY 5	apple slices ✓	3 per participant	X _____	= _____
	brown sugar ✓	1 tablespoon per participant	X _____	= _____
	cream cheese ✓	1 tablespoon per participant	X _____	= _____
	milk ✓	about 1 teaspoon per participant	X _____	= _____
	water or juice	1 quart for every 5 participants	X _____	= _____

PLANNING

SERVING SUPPLIES

Item	Required Amount	Total Number of Participants	Total Required Amount
paper plates	3 per participant	X _____	= _____ paper plates
paper cups	5 per participant	X _____	= _____ paper cups
napkins	5 per participant	X _____	= _____ napkins
plastic spoons	1 per participant	X _____	= _____ plastic spoons
snack-size resealable bags	4 per participant	X _____	= _____ snack-size resealable bags
pitchers	1 for every 5 participants	X _____	= _____ pitchers
paper muffin cups	2 per participant	X _____	= _____ paper muffin cups
hand wipes	5 per participant	X _____	= _____ hand wipes

CHUCK WAGON CHOW SERVICE CREW SUPPLIES

Item	Required Amount	Total Number of Ranch Crews in the Service Crew (¼ total of Ranch Crews)	Total Amonut Required
plastic knives	2 per Ranch Crew	X _____	= _____
resealable sandwich bags	4 per Ranch Crew	X _____	= _____

OTHER SUPPLIES

- [ ] Wrangler Ringer* or other attention-getting signal
- [ ] antibacterial soap, hand gel, or individually wrapped hand wipes
- [ ] 2 or 3 rolls of paper towels
- [ ] assortment of serving bowls, plates, trays, and utensils
- [ ] trash cans or trash bags
- [ ] *Sing & Play Stampede Music* CD* (optional)
- [ ] CD player (optional)
- [ ] 1 Wild Ride Bible Guide* (for an example)

I think I'll rope me one of those tasty snacks!

*available from Group Publishing and your local Group supplier

PLANNING

BONUS IDEA!

One church we visited had a smart way to ensure they got the correct supplies. Near their donation list, they included a digital photograph of what less-familiar items (such as paint markers) looked like. That way, there were no misunderstandings and they were able to get all the correct supplies the first time!

This great tip comes from churches that have fine-tuned the art of collecting VBS supplies. It just doesn't get any easier!

1. Photocopy the "Join the Stampede!" sign below on colored paper. Designate a different color of paper for each station—for example, blue paper for Cowpoke Crafts, orange paper for Chuck Wagon Chow, and red paper for Prairie Dog Preschool.

2. Fill in the information on each "cow." Indicate whether the item needs to be donated (items that will be used up, such as food) or borrowed (items that can be returned, such as a bucket).

3. Cut out the cows, and post them on a bulletin board in a high-traffic area of your church. Make an announcement to inform church members that they can take items from the board and donate the requested items.

4. As items are delivered to the specified area, sort them by the color of the attached paper. Just before Avalanche Ranch begins, collect the papers and sort them into donated and borrowed items.

5. After VBS, simply have station leaders retrieve the borrowed items. Match the items with their slips of paper, and return the items to their owners.

JOIN THE STAMPEDE!

Item Needed: _____

Donated   Borrowed

Avalanche Ranch Director:

_____

Phone: _____

Your Name: _____

Phone: _____

Please return this item to me by _____

Please attach this cow to the item

and deliver it to _____

by _____ (date).

THANK YOU!

DAILY SCHEDULES

Each day when kids come to Avalanche Ranch, they visit seven stations. All Ranch Crews visit Sing & Play Stampede, Chuck Wagon Chow, and Showtime Roundup together. In between these activities, the remaining stations run simultaneously. Station leaders repeat their activities four times, with a different group of Ranch Crews each time. When it's time for groups to move to a new station, walk through Avalanche Ranch and sound the Wrangler Ringer. This helps kids, crew leaders, and station leaders stay on schedule.

After you've assigned kids to Ranch Crews, you should assign Ranch Crews to groups. Each group consists of one-fourth of the elementary-age Ranch Crews at Avalanche Ranch. To eliminate confusion with Ranch Crew numbers, use letters, colors, or ranch-animal names to label these four groups.

For example, if you have 35 kids, you will end up with seven Ranch Crews of five kids. You will put all seven Ranch Crews into one large group. The large group will travel to the stations together. (See sample schedule on page 27.)

If you have 60 kids, you will end up with 12 Ranch Crews of five kids. You will then assign the crews to larger groups in this way:

A—crews 1-3	C—crews 7-9
B—crews 4-6	D—crews 10-12

If you have 150 kids, you'll end up with 30 Ranch Crews of five kids. You will then assign the crews to larger groups in this way:

A—crews 1-7	C—crews 16-22
B—crews 8-15	D—crews 23-30

If you have more than 150 kids, it's important to set up double stations for Horseplay Games, Wild Bible Adventures, Cowpoke Crafts and Missions, and Chadder's Wild West Theater. (If you don't set up double stations, you'll have too many kids in one station at a time.) For more information on running double stations, see the diagram on page 28.

You'll notice on the "Daily Schedule and Announcements" pages (pp. 87-96) that groups visit the stations in a different order each day. This schedule shift provides welcome variety for kids and allows a different group to perform Chuck Wagon Chow Service each day. Chuck Wagon Chow Service is extremely important to the crews, who get a chance to share God's love.

Preschool children will keep the same schedule each day but will perform Chuck Wagon Chow Service on Day 1. Preschoolers will leave their room and join older kids for Sing & Play Stampede and Showtime Roundup. All other preschool activities take place in or near the Prairie Dog Preschool room.

Field Test Findings We discovered that it's a good idea to arrange your Ranch Crews so that you have *at least* one experienced adult crew leader in each lettered group. Adults can offer encouragement, leadership, or helpful advice to younger crew leaders.

Field Test Findings It always happens on Day 2: Someone looks at the schedule and protests, "This is the same schedule as yesterday!" Actually, it's not. The elementary kids *do* rotate in the same order, but one group will have Chuck Wagon Chow Service instead of Horseplay Games. Since preschoolers have Chuck Wagon Chow Service on Day 1, there's no need for the schedule to change until Day 3.

PLANNING

Our crew leaders asked for more "talk-starters" on their daily schedules so they could really get to know the kids in their crews. So we've made these schedules two-sided: The daily schedule is on the front, and a few fun jokes and activities for crews are on the back! There's even room for you to add your own creative ideas!

Use the sample morning and evening schedules (pp. 85-86) to plan your VBS times. Each day before Avalanche Ranch, fill in the appropriate day's schedule (pp. 87-96) with times and announcements. Then photocopy both sides of the schedule, and distribute the schedule. (To avoid confusion, you might want to photocopy each day's schedule on a different color of paper.) Don't forget to give copies to the Ranch Crew Leaders!

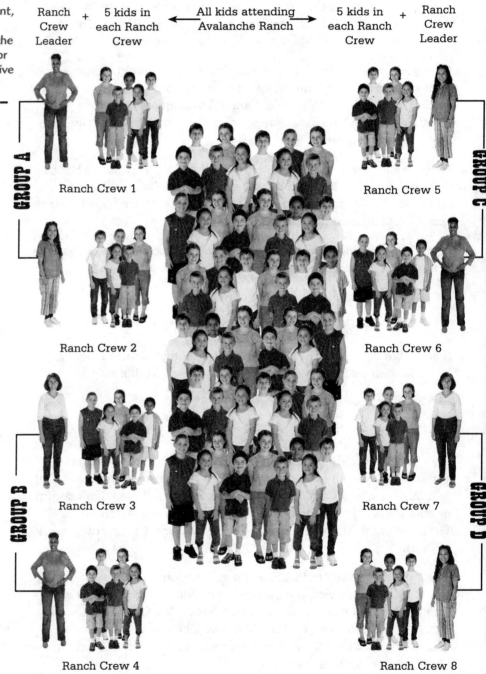

Ranch Crew Leader + 5 kids in each Ranch Crew ← All kids attending Avalanche Ranch → 5 kids in each Ranch Crew + Ranch Crew Leader

GROUP A

GROUP B

GROUP C

GROUP D

Ranch Crew 1

Ranch Crew 2

Ranch Crew 3

Ranch Crew 4

Ranch Crew 5

Ranch Crew 6

Ranch Crew 7

Ranch Crew 8

PLANNING

SAMPLE DAY 1 SCHEDULE

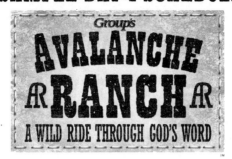

Morning Schedule (8:30-11:30)

Time	Group A Crews 1-5	Group B Crews 6-10	Group C Crews 11-15	Group D Crews 16-20	Preschool
8:30-8:55	Sing & Play Stampede	Sing & Play Stampede	Sing & Play Stampede	Sing & Play Stampede	Prairie Dog Preschool
Allow five minutes to move to your next Ranch Station.					
9:00-9:20	Wild Bible Adventures	Cowpoke Crafts and Missions	Horseplay Games	Chadder's Wild West Theater	Chuck Wagon Chow Service
Allow five minutes to move to your next Ranch Station.					
9:25-9:45	Cowpoke Crafts and Missions	Horseplay Games	Chadder's Wild West Theater	Wild Bible Adventures	Prairie Dog Preschool
Allow five minutes to move to your next Ranch Station.					
9:50-10:10	Chuck Wagon Chow	Chuck Wagon Chow	Chuck Wagon Chow	Chuck Wagon Chow	Chuck Wagon Chow
Allow five minutes to move to your next Ranch Station.					
10:15-10:35	Horseplay Games	Chadder's Wild West Theater	Wild Bible Adventures	Cowpoke Crafts and Missions	Prairie Dog Preschool
Allow five minutes to move to your next Ranch Station.					
10:40-11:00	Chadder's Wild West Theater	Wild Bible Adventures	Cowpoke Crafts and Missions	Horseplay Games	Prairie Dog Preschool
Allow five minutes to move to your next Ranch Station.					
11:05-11:30	Showtime Roundup	Showtime Roundup	Showtime Roundup	Showtime Roundup	Showtime Roundup

PLANNING

SAMPLE DAY 1 SCHEDULE

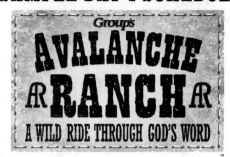

Evening Schedule (6:00-9:00)*

Time	Group A Crews 1-5	Group B Crews 6-10	Group C Crews 11-15	Group D Crews 16-20	Preschool
6:00-6:25	Sing & Play Stampede	Sing & Play Stampede	Sing & Play Stampede	Sing & Play Stampede	Prairie Dog Preschool
Allow five minutes to move to your next Ranch Station.					
6:30-6:50	Wild Bible Adventures	Cowpoke Crafts and Missions	Horseplay Games	Chadder's Wild West Theater	Chuck Wagon Chow Service
Allow five minutes to move to your next Ranch Station.					
6:55-7:15	Cowpoke Crafts and Missions	Horseplay Games	Chadder's Wild West Theater	Wild Bible Adventures	Prairie Dog Preschool
Allow five minutes to move to your next Ranch Station.					
7:20-7:40	Chuck Wagon Chow	Chuck Wagon Chow	Chuck Wagon Chow	Chuck Wagon Chow	Chuck Wagon Chow
Allow five minutes to move to your next Ranch Station.					
7:45-8:05	Horseplay Games	Chadder's Wild West Theater	Wild Bible Adventures	Cowpoke Crafts and Missions	Prairie Dog Preschool
Allow five minutes to move to your next Ranch Station.					
8:10-8:30	Chadder's Wild West Theater	Wild Bible Adventures	Cowpoke Crafts and Missions	Horseplay Games	Prairie Dog Preschool
Allow five minutes to move to your next Ranch Station.					
8:35-9:00	Showtime Roundup	Showtime Roundup	Showtime Roundup	Showtime Roundup	Showtime Roundup

*Kids will need *at least* 20 minutes to complete each station. If you need to end your program promptly at 9 p.m., shorten your "move" time to two or three minutes between each station.

PLANNING

BIBLE POINT
God is real.

TREASURE VERSE
"The Lord is the only true God"
(Jeremiah 10:10).

BIBLE STORY
Rahab protects the Israelite spies
(Joshua 2).

Group's
AVALANCHE RANCH
A WILD RIDE THROUGH GOD'S WORD

Daily Schedule and Announcements

Time	Group A Crews _____	Group B Crews _____	Group C Crews _____	Group D Crews _____	Preschool
	Sing & Play Stampede	Sing & Play Stampede	Sing & Play Stampede	Sing & Play Stampede	Prairie Dog Preschool
	Allow five minutes to move to your next Ranch Station.				
	Wild Bible Adventures	Cowpoke Crafts and Missions	Horseplay Games	Chadder's Wild West Theater	Chuck Wagon Chow Service
	Allow five minutes to move to your next Ranch Station.				
	Cowpoke Crafts and Missions	Horseplay Games	Chadder's Wild West Theater	Wild Bible Adventures	Prairie Dog Preschool
	Allow five minutes to move to your next Ranch Station.				
	Chuck Wagon Chow	Chuck Wagon Chow	Chuck Wagon Chow	Chuck Wagon Chow	Chuck Wagon Chow
	Allow five minutes to move to your next Ranch Station.				
	Horseplay Games	Chadder's Wild West Theater	Wild Bible Adventures	Cowpoke Crafts and Missions	Prairie Dog Preschool
	Allow five minutes to move to your next Ranch Station.				
	Chadder's Wild West Theater	Wild Bible Adventures	Cowpoke Crafts and Missions	Horseplay Games	Prairie Dog Preschool
	Allow five minutes to move to your next Ranch Station.				
	Showtime Roundup	Showtime Roundup	Showtime Roundup	Showtime Roundup	Showtime Roundup

Today's Announcements:

> In Rasario, Argentina, horses are required to wear hats in hot weather.

SILLY STAMPEDE

Horses move at four different speeds: walk, trot, canter, and gallop. Let each crew member demonstrate what each of these "gaits" looks like. (The rest of the group can make clip-clopping sound effects!)

A mule is a mix of a horse and a donkey. Can you mix two animals to create a new one? What would your new animal do? What would you call it?

HOW DOES BUC'S SISTER WEAR HER HAIR?

In a pony tail

Today's Bible story is about two spies.
Be spies right now!
Look around and see if you can spy the following:

- three cowboy hats
- a mountain
- two people who are laughing
- five people wearing cowboy boots
- the crew wearing the most green

ASK

STATION LEADERS:
Tell about a time when you rode a horse (it's OK if it was a stick horse or rocking horse).

WHAT DID BUC TAKE WHEN HE HAD A COLD?

Cough stirrup

DAY 2

BIBLE POINT
God is with us.

TREASURE VERSE
"For the Lord your God is with you wherever you go" (Joshua 1:9).

BIBLE STORY
The Israelites cross the Jordan River (Joshua 3–4).

Group's
AVALANCHE RANCH
A WILD RIDE THROUGH GOD'S WORD

Daily Schedule and Announcements

Time	Group A Crews _____	Group B Crews _____	Group C Crews _____	Group D Crews _____	Preschool
	Sing & Play Stampede	Sing & Play Stampede	Sing & Play Stampede	Sing & Play Stampede	Prairie Dog Preschool
	Allow five minutes to move to your next Ranch Station.				
	Wild Bible Adventures	Cowpoke Crafts and Missions	Chuck Wagon Chow Service	Chadder's Wild West Theater	Prairie Dog Preschool
	Allow five minutes to move to your next Ranch Station.				
	Cowpoke Crafts and Missions	Horseplay Games	Chadder's Wild West Theater	Wild Bible Adventures	Prairie Dog Preschool
	Allow five minutes to move to your next Ranch Station.				
	Chuck Wagon Chow	Chuck Wagon Chow	Chuck Wagon Chow	Chuck Wagon Chow	Chuck Wagon Chow
	Allow five minutes to move to your next Ranch Station.				
	Horseplay Games	Chadder's Wild West Theater	Wild Bible Adventures	Cowpoke Crafts and Missions	Prairie Dog Preschool
	Allow five minutes to move to your next Ranch Station.				
	Chadder's Wild West Theater	Wild Bible Adventures	Cowpoke Crafts and Missions	Horseplay Games	Prairie Dog Preschool
	Allow five minutes to move to your next Ranch Station.				
	Showtime Roundup	Showtime Roundup	Showtime Roundup	Showtime Roundup	Showtime Roundup

Today's Announcements:

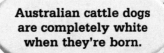

Australian cattle dogs are completely white when they're born.

SILLY STAMPEDE

WHICH OF SHADOW'S PUPPY FRIENDS LIKES TO TAKE BATHS?

A shampoodle

A cattle dog is a cowboy's best friend. Who is your best frie

What are three words you'd use to describe your best frien

What wacky shadows can you make?
See who can make a shadow of...

- an alligator
- a bear
- a flower
- a pine tree
- Chadder

ASK
STATION LEADERS:
What is one thing you always keep with you?

WHAT DOES SHADOW LIKE BEST FOR BREAKFAST?

Pooched eggs

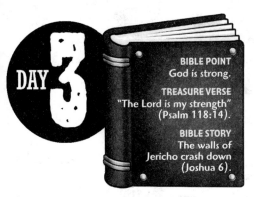

DAY 3

BIBLE POINT
God is strong.

TREASURE VERSE
"The Lord is my strength"
(Psalm 118:14).

BIBLE STORY
The walls of
Jericho crash down
(Joshua 6).

Daily Schedule
and Announcements

Time	Group B Crews _____	Group C Crews _____	Group D Crews _____	Group A Crews _____	Preschool
	Sing & Play Stampede	Sing & Play Stampede	Sing & Play Stampede	Sing & Play Stampede	Prairie Dog Preschool
Allow five minutes to move to your next Ranch Station.					
	Wild Bible Adventures	Cowpoke Crafts and Missions	Chuck Wagon Chow Service	Chadder's Wild West Theater	Prairie Dog Preschool
Allow five minutes to move to your next Ranch Station.					
	Cowpoke Crafts and Missions	Horseplay Games	Chadder's Wild West Theater	Wild Bible Adventures	Prairie Dog Preschool
Allow five minutes to move to your next Ranch Station.					
	Chuck Wagon Chow	Chuck Wagon Chow	Chuck Wagon Chow	Chuck Wagon Chow	Chuck Wagon Chow
Allow five minutes to move to your next Ranch Station.					
	Horseplay Games	Chadder's Wild West Theater	Wild Bible Adventures	Cowpoke Crafts and Missions	Prairie Dog Preschool
Allow five minutes to move to your next Ranch Station.					
	Chadder's Wild West Theater	Wild Bible Adventures	Cowpoke Crafts and Missions	Horseplay Games	Prairie Dog Preschool
Allow five minutes to move to your next Ranch Station.					
	Showtime Roundup	Showtime Roundup	Showtime Roundup	Showtime Roundup	Showtime Roundup

Today's Announcements:

Believe it or not,
the American Bison
is a good swimmer!

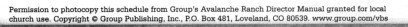

SILLY STAMPEDE

When the Israelites shouted, the wall around Jericho just toppled over! Wow! What do you think would happen if your entire crew shouted? This might be one activity you *don't* want to try! Instead, make up a silly cheer for your crew.

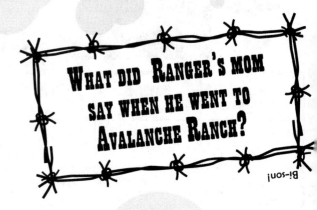

WHAT DID RANGER'S MOM SAY WHEN HE WENT TO AVALANCHE RANCH?

Bi-son!

Bison, like Ranger, like to take dust baths. Does that sound more fun than a regular bath? If you could take a bath in something other than water, what would it be and why?

Make up a song about Avalanche Ranch, to the tune of "Home on the Ra We'll even start you off:

Av-Ava-lanche Ranch Where the...

STATION LEADERS: What's something that makes you yell really loud?

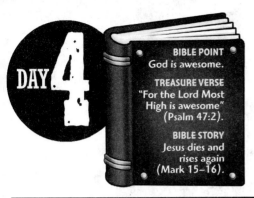

BIBLE POINT
God is awesome.

TREASURE VERSE
"For the Lord Most High is awesome"
(Psalm 47:2).

BIBLE STORY
Jesus dies and rises again
(Mark 15–16).

Daily Schedule and Announcements

Time	Group C Crews _____	Group D Crews _____	Group A Crews _____	Group B Crews _____	Preschool
	Sing & Play Stampede	Sing & Play Stampede	Sing & Play Stampede	Sing & Play Stampede	Prairie Dog Preschool
	Allow five minutes to move to your next Ranch Station.				
	Wild Bible Adventures	Cowpoke Crafts and Missions	Chuck Wagon Chow Service	Chadder's Wild West Theater	Prairie Dog Preschool
	Allow five minutes to move to your next Ranch Station.				
	Cowpoke Crafts and Missions	Horseplay Games	Chadder's Wild West Theater	Wild Bible Adventures	Prairie Dog Preschool
	Allow five minutes to move to your next Ranch Station.				
	Chuck Wagon Chow	Chuck Wagon Chow	Chuck Wagon Chow	Chuck Wagon Chow	Chuck Wagon Chow
	Allow five minutes to move to your next Ranch Station.				
	Horseplay Games	Chadder's Wild West Theater	Wild Bible Adventures	Cowpoke Crafts and Missions	Prairie Dog Preschool
	Allow five minutes to move to your next Ranch Station.				
	Chadder's Wild West Theater	Wild Bible Adventures	Cowpoke Crafts and Missions	Horseplay Games	Prairie Dog Preschool
	Allow five minutes to move to your next Ranch Station.				
	Showtime Roundup	Showtime Roundup	Showtime Roundup	Showtime Roundup	Showtime Roundup

Today's Announcements:

Bald eagles aren't really bald—they just have white feathers on their heads.

SILLY STAMPEDE

Bald eagles like their homes—they may even use the same nest again and again. One eagle's nest had been around for 34 years and weighed about 4000 pounds! That's as much as two small cars! What do you like the best about your home?

ASK STATION LEADERS:
What's the most awesome thing you've ever seen?

Eagles are kind of like Superman—they can fly and have awesome eyesight. Which superhero would you like to be? Why?

Who in your crew acts most like a...

bucking bronco? (Find someone with lots of energy.)

cattle dog? (Look for someone who keeps everyone together)

bison? (This person might be very strong.)

eagle? (Who seems to fly from one thing to another?)

prairie dog? (You might find someone who's quiet.)

DAY 5

BIBLE POINT
God is in charge.

TREASURE VERSE
"If you love me, obey my commandments" (John 14:15).

BIBLE STORY
God heals Naaman (2 Kings 5).

Group's
AVALANCHE RANCH
A WILD RIDE THROUGH GOD'S WORD

Daily Schedule and Announcements

Time	Group D Crews _____	Group A Crews _____	Group B Crews _____	Group C Crews _____	Preschool
	Sing & Play Stampede	Sing & Play Stampede	Sing & Play Stampede	Sing & Play Stampede	Prairie Dog Preschool
	Allow five minutes to move to your next Ranch Station.				
	Wild Bible Adventures	Cowpoke Crafts and Missions	Chuck Wagon Chow Service	Chadder's Wild West Theater	Prairie Dog Preschool
	Allow five minutes to move to your next Ranch Station.				
	Cowpoke Crafts and Missions	Horseplay Games	Chadder's Wild West Theater	Wild Bible Adventures	Prairie Dog Preschool
	Allow five minutes to move to your next Ranch Station.				
	Chuck Wagon Chow	Chuck Wagon Chow	Chuck Wagon Chow	Chuck Wagon Chow	Chuck Wagon Chow
	Allow five minutes to move to your next Ranch Station.				
	Horseplay Games	Chadder's Wild West Theater	Wild Bible Adventures	Cowpoke Crafts and Missions	Prairie Dog Preschool
	Allow five minutes to move to your next Ranch Station.				
	Chadder's Wild West Theater	Wild Bible Adventures	Cowpoke Crafts and Missions	Horseplay Games	Prairie Dog Preschool
	Allow five minutes to move to your next Ranch Station.				
	Showtime Roundup	Showtime Roundup	Showtime Roundup	Showtime Roundup	Showtime Roundup

Today's Announcements:

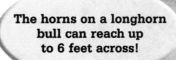

The horns on a longhorn bull can reach up to 6 feet across!

SILLY STAMPEDE

WHAT DO YOU CALL A SLEEPING BULL?

A bull-dozer

What was your most favorite part Avalanche Ranch?

1 THING

Tell each crew member one thing you like about him or her.

WHAT GAME DOES BOSS LIKE TO PLAY AT BIRTHDAY PARTIES?

Moosical chairs

STATION LEADERS:

Find a different way to thank each station leader. You might give high fives, hugs, or say "You're cool!"

Recruiting for Avalanche Ranch

These great recruiting ideas will start a stampede to Avalanche Ranch!

A SURVIVAL GUIDE TO RECRUITING

You love VBS, right? You love watching kids' faces light up as they worship. You love preparing awesome Bible adventures for kids to take part in. You actually dream of wild, elaborate decorations for your VBS theme. And you'll be the first to admit that VBS crafts are right up your alley. But you get a little worried when it comes to recruiting. "Where will I find leaders for all these kids?" It's true that finding all the right volunteers to pull off a successful VBS program *can* be a challenge.

That's why we're here to help! You see, recruiting doesn't *have* to be a headache. It can actually be a fun, energizing opportunity to connect with people who have a passion for children's ministry—people just like you! We're here to help you find all the station leaders and Ranch Crew Leaders you need for your Avalanche Ranch VBS. (You might even find additional registration staff, photographers, decorating specialists, and maybe a co-director!) So prowl through these pages and discover just how fun—and effective—your recruiting efforts can be!

This year recruiting can be even easier! That's because we've provided you with two bonus tools to help you find all the volunteers you need for a great adventure. The *Wah-hoo!* DVD includes three brief "commercials" that will have everyone signing up to help with Avalanche Ranch. You can also use your VBS Web Toybox to send job descriptions and to allow volunteers to apply for positions online. For more information, check out your Avalanche Ranch catalog or visit www.group.com/vbs.

Wow! Recruiting the whole pack is easy with all the ways Group helps you find volunteers!

ROUNDING UP RANCH STAFF

RANCH STATION LEADERS

Station leaders are the core of Avalanche Ranch. These are the people who teach and show Jesus' love to the kids who attend your program. Kids look forward to seeing the station leaders each day, and so do you! You need at least eight volunteers—one leader for each of the following stations:

- Sing & Play Stampede

- Cowpoke Crafts and Missions

- Horseplay Games

- Chuck Wagon Chow

- Spotlight Drama (optional)

- Wild Bible Adventures

- Chadder's Wild West Theater

- Showtime Roundup

- Prairie Dog Preschool

(If you choose to do Spotlight Drama, you'll also need a Spotlight Drama Leader, who will take pictures of kids in certain poses that coordinate with a slick PowerPoint slide show.)

Your Prairie Dog Preschool Director will help you recruit four additional leaders for the following Prairie Dog stations:

- Bible Adventures and Missions

- Craft and Play

- Chadder's Theater

- Games

If you're expecting more than 150 kids to attend Avalanche Ranch, it's important that you double up on station leaders. Purchase an additional leader manual for each station, and run two sessions of each station simultaneously. This will help keep station group sizes manageable (fewer than 30 kids per session) and guarantee success for your leaders.

If you have fewer than 40 children, your job is even easier! Form Ranch Crews, and then have all the Ranch Crews travel together in one group. (See the schedule and setup on page 26.) This way, station leaders need to teach their stations only one time. Or station leaders may want to teach more than one station, making your recruiting efforts a snap!

Field Test Findings Our station leaders who took the team teaching approach were glad they did. They reduced their planning time and shared the task of bringing in supplies and setting up. Not only was it easier for them to manage fewer kids in each session, but they simply liked having a friend to work with. (Plus, we've found that adults love the program as much as the kids!)

Trail Tip

If you want to appoint an assistant director, ask the Sing & Play Stampede Leader or Showtime Roundup Leader. Because these two leaders present their material only once each day, they'll be free to help you handle last-minute details. (These two stations can even be led by the same person.)

Field Test Findings

Talk about easy recruiting! After our field test, several station leaders volunteered to lead their areas next year. Other churches have reported similar results, with a high volunteer return rate. One director of a VBS of 600 kids said she delighted in sitting back and watching last year's volunteers recruit this year's!

A local pastor said he kind of missed being more involved. It seemed that the director volunteered to lead next year's VBS as soon as this summer's program was over. He had never seen anything like it!

Station leaders should be adults or mature older teenagers. You'll find a specific job description for each station leader in the following pages. In general, you should look for station leaders who are

- dependable church members or regular attendees,
- enthusiastic about working with children,
- excited about serving at Avalanche Ranch,
- patient and kind,
- good communicators,
- comfortable speaking in front of groups of 30 or more, and
- gifted in their station areas.

In more traditional VBS models, volunteers prepare and teach everything from games and Bible lessons to crafts and more. That's why your volunteers will *love* being station leaders: because they can lead out of their gifts, interests, and abilities. Plus, each station leader manual is easy to follow, providing lists of easy-to-collect supplies and field-tested activities.

Use the details in the job descriptions (pp. 106-118) to help you enlist leaders for the stations. Give each leader a copy of his or her job description, and offer to address any questions or concerns that may arise. Invite station leaders and Ranch Crew Leaders to your scheduled leader training.

If you're using VBS Web Toybox, you can compile a list of station leaders and their information in your database.

Or list the names, addresses, and phone numbers of your station leaders in the chart on page 101 so that you're able to quickly access the information. Use the chart on page 102 for your Prairie Dog Preschool staff.

RECRUITING

RANCH STATION LEADERS

STATION	LEADER'S NAME	ADDRESS	PHONE NUMBER	E-MAIL ADDRESS	OTHER NOTES
Sing & Play Stampede					
Cowpoke Crafts and Missions					
Horseplay Games					
Chuck Wagon Chow					
Wild Bible Adventures					
Chadder's Wild West Theater					
Showtime Roundup					
Spotlight Drama					

Prairie Dog Preschool LEADERS

STATION	LEADER'S NAME	ADDRESS	PHONE NUMBER	E-MAIL ADDRESS	OTHER NOTES
Director					
Bible Adventures and Missions					
Craft and Play					
Chadder's Theater					
Games					

RANCH CREW LEADERS

After you've enlisted station leaders, you'll need a group of Ranch Crew Leaders. The Ranch Crew Leader is an important part of each Ranch Crew. Anyone in your church who loves the Lord and loves children can be a Ranch Crew Leader! You'll need one Ranch Crew Leader for every five elementary-age children.

Ranch Crew Leaders don't have to prepare anything; they just come each day, guide their crew members through activities, help facilitate discussions, and generally join in the Avalanche Ranch fun. Their week will go more smoothly if you have a brief orientation meeting with your Ranch Crew Leaders or invite them to your leader training meeting. The *Wah-hoo!* DVD has special training tips just for them. It gives them helpful hints on leading discussions and solving any problems that might arise among their crews. We've also included photocopiable handouts that orient Ranch Crew Leaders with the teaching style at Avalanche Ranch and give them some ideas for capitalizing on extra time. You can find these handouts in the leader training section of this manual (pp. 139-142).

A Ranch Crew Leader is

- a friend and a helper.
- responsible for drawing kids into discussions, as much as possible.
- someone who offers kids choices.
- someone who asks questions.
- someone who encourages kids.
- someone who helps and encourages station leaders.

Photocopy the "Join the Avalanche Ranch Team" sign (p. 119), and post it in your church lobby. You'll be pleasantly surprised at how many Ranch Crew Leaders join your team!

Field Test Findings We highly recommend a Crew Leader Coordinator position—a person responsible to help train, support, and guide crew leaders. Since crew leaders play such an important role at your program, it's a great idea to give extra support and time to these awesome volunteers.

Trail Tip If crew leaders can't attend the leader training meeting, encourage them to watch the *Wah-hoo!* DVD and review their Crew Leader Pocket Guides. To allow plenty of time for crew leaders to understand their roles, you might distribute the Crew Leader Pocket Guides several weeks before your Avalanche Ranch. Your job will be much easier if crew leaders read and understand this information well before the adventure begins.

HOW DO I BEGIN RECRUITING?

Remember, God's in charge!

First, take a deep breath. Now…pray. Remember, Jesus knows each person in your church and each child who will attend your Avalanche Ranch. So ask Jesus to open the eyes, hearts, and minds of those who will be just the right "fit" for your program.

Next, get the word out! (This is the fun part!) Let folks know that this is more than "your grandfather's VBS." Prayerfully determine the number of children you would like to reach with Avalanche Ranch, and don't be afraid to think big! Then share your vision in a creative way.

For example, if your goal is to have 100 kids attend Avalanche Ranch, you might decorate a large sheet of bulletin board paper with 100 paper horses. Add the heading, "Let's corral 100 kids at Avalanche Ranch!" Leave this bulletin board up for a few weeks to get everyone excited about what's coming.

Get gallopin', and make a visual impact!

 **Trail Tip**

A multisensory, multimedia approach could bring many additional volunteers. Set out some of the sample Chuck Wagon Chow snacks near your sign-up area. Have a TV/DVD player nearby, and play the *Wah-hoo!* DVD or the *Sing & Play Stampede Music* video or DVD. If you've used a Group VBS in the past, videotape a few volunteers or kids telling what they liked best about it. You'll attract plenty of potential volunteers!

Let's corral 100 kids at Avalanche Ranch!

Share your eagle-eye vision for ministry!

Write out your vision, and then tell how people can make this vision a reality. Using the bulletin board idea, you might simply add the words "And *You* Can Help Make That Happen!" to the bottom of your bulletin board. Surround your board with job descriptions—people will be amazed at the fun and creative ways they can get involved with this program! If you've used a Group VBS program before, you might even print out some great testimonials. Post these next to the job descriptions as a way to show *everyone* that VBS can be a blast!

RECRUITING

You don't need to nag people, but keep your vision out in front of people at all times. Rather than making a negative plea for help ("I know nobody really wants to help, but…"), state your needs simply. You might say, "Our goal is to reach 100 children with Jesus' love at Avalanche Ranch. Right now we have enough volunteers to reach 50 kids. How can you help?" Visually remind people of your goal. If you use the "corral" bulletin board, you might slip a few paper horseshoes into the church bulletin.

Roam the range to meet people face to face!

Experienced VBS directors will tell you that there's no substitute for the personal touch. (Plus, it's harder for people to turn you down face to face!) If you truly think someone would be a dynamite Ranch Crew Leader, tell him or her! If, after the youth Christmas drama, you see a teenager who would be a great help in Wild Bible Adventures, let him or her know! One director tells us that he goes through the church telephone directory line by line, prayerfully considering *each* person. It has been a super way to involve those who don't naturally come to mind! (With the e-mail service in your Web Toybox, you can even e-mail job descriptions or letters to those who might be excellent Avalanche Ranch staff members!)

Be a friend. Treat volunteers with thoughtfulness and respect!

Your volunteers are valuable. (Of course, you knew that!) So be sure to treat each one with thoughtfulness and respect. If someone volunteers for a position that you don't feel is a good "fit," gently recommend another place he or she might better serve. In our field tests, we've had Ranch Crew Leaders who would have been much better assistant station leaders, preschool crew leaders, or other helpers. Check out pages 123-124 for a list of other ways to use people's gifts and abilities to ensure that Avalanche Ranch is a positive experience for everyone!

SING & PLAY STAMPEDE LEADER

RELATED INTERESTS

You'll enjoy leading Sing & Play Stampede if you enjoy any of the following activities:

- playing a musical instrument,
- directing or singing in your church choir,
- leading worship, and
- acting or drama.

QUALIFICATIONS

You'll be a successful Sing & Play Stampede Leader if you

- love the Lord and love children,
- have experience leading songs or singing with children,
- can motivate and energize kids, and
- are comfortable speaking in front of large groups.

RESPONSIBILITIES

As a Sing & Play Stampede Leader, you'll be responsible for

- attending scheduled leader training,
- repeating the daily Bible Point as you teach,
- learning the music and motions for 10 Avalanche Ranch songs,
- teaching kids the words and motions to several songs each day,
- asking kids to share about their Daily Challenges,
- leading singing for the entire VBS,
- assisting with Showtime Roundup program each day, and
- assisting the Avalanche Ranch Director as needed.

JOIN THE WILD RIDE AT AVALANCHE RANCH!

Job Description

COWPOKE CRAFTS AND MISSIONS LEADER

RELATED INTERESTS

You'll enjoy leading Cowpoke Crafts and Missions if you enjoy any of the following activities:

- 🐾 watching kids have a great time,
- 🐾 missions and international outreach,
- 🐾 arts and crafts, and
- 🐾 working with your hands.

QUALIFICATIONS

You'll be a successful Cowpoke Crafts and Missions Leader if you

- 🐾 love the Lord and love children,
- 🐾 are creative and fun-loving,
- 🐾 can give clear directions to children, and
- 🐾 show patience while working with lots of children.

RESPONSIBILITIES

As a Cowpoke Crafts and Missions Leader, you'll be responsible for

- 🐾 attending scheduled leader training,
- 🐾 collecting necessary supplies,
- 🐾 preparing sample Bible Point Crafts before Avalanche Ranch,
- 🐾 repeating the daily Bible Point as you teach,
- 🐾 helping children create one-of-a-kind crafts,
- 🐾 helping kids carry out their Operation Kid-to-Kid mission, and
- 🐾 leading four sessions of Cowpoke Crafts and Missions each day.

JOIN THE WILD RIDE AT AVALANCHE RANCH!

Job Description

HORSEPLAY GAMES LEADER

RELATED INTERESTS

You'll enjoy leading Horseplay Games if you enjoy any of the following activities:

- team sports,
- outdoor recreational activities, and
- encouraging others to do their best.

QUALIFICATIONS

You'll be a successful Horseplay Games Leader if you

- love the Lord and love children;
- enjoy playing games;
- are positive, active, and energetic; and
- can organize and motivate children.

RESPONSIBILITIES

As a Horseplay Games Leader, you'll be responsible for

- attending scheduled leader training,
- repeating the daily Bible Point as you teach,
- collecting necessary supplies for Horseplay Games,
- clearly explaining each game,
- assisting the Spotlight Drama Leader, and
- leading three sessions of Horseplay Games each day.

JOIN THE WILD RIDE AT AVALANCHE RANCH!

Job Description

SPOTLIGHT DRAMA LEADER

RELATED INTERESTS

You'll enjoy leading Spotlight Drama if you enjoy any of the following activities:

- photography,
- computer graphics, and
- creating mulitmedia presentations.

QUALIFICATIONS

You'll be a successful Spotlight Drama Leader if you

- love the Lord and love children;
- enjoy photography;
- are positive, active, and energetic; and
- can organize and motivate children.

RESPONSIBILITIES

As a Spotlight Drama Leader, you'll be responsible for

- attending scheduled leader training,
- repeating the daily Bible Point as you teach,
- collecting necessary supplies for Spotlight Drama,
- taking pictures of children in specific poses (according to a script),
- copying the photos into a special PowerPoint slide show, and
- setting up equipment to show the Spotlight Drama during each day's Showtime Roundup.

JOIN THE WILD RIDE AT AVALANCHE RANCH!

Job Description

CHUCK WAGON CHOW LEADER

RELATED INTERESTS

You'll enjoy leading Chuck Wagon Chow if you enjoy any of the following activities:

- preparing and serving food,
- maintaining a clean environment,
- working in a kitchen or restaurant, and
- organizing and supervising teams of people.

QUALIFICATIONS

You'll be a successful Chuck Wagon Chow Leader if you

- love the Lord and love children,
- enjoy cooking and food preparation,
- believe children can accomplish big tasks,
- can give clear directions to children, and
- accept and encourage children's abilities.

RESPONSIBILITIES

As a Chuck Wagon Chow Leader, you'll be responsible for

- attending scheduled leader training,
- repeating the daily Bible Point as you teach,
- coordinating food supplies for each day's snack,
- setting up assembly lines to help kids prepare each day's snack,
- serving snacks to the entire Avalanche Ranch, and
- cleaning up the Chuck Wagon Chow area after snacks are served.

JOIN THE WILD RIDE AT AVALANCHE RANCH!

WILD BIBLE ADVENTURES LEADER

RELATED INTERESTS

You'll enjoy leading Wild Bible Adventures if you enjoy any of the following activities:

- storytelling,
- acting or drama,
- leading discussions, and
- surprising others.

QUALIFICATIONS

You'll be a successful Wild Bible Adventures Leader if you

- love the Lord and love children;
- have a flair for drama and can play a role convincingly;
- relish a fast-paced, exciting atmosphere;
- believe in hands-on discovery as a learning technique; and
- feel comfortable facilitating group discussions.

RESPONSIBILITIES

As a Wild Bible Adventures Leader, you'll be responsible for

- attending scheduled leader training,
- repeating the daily Bible Point as you teach,
- collecting necessary supplies,
- recruiting three volunteers to perform simple roles as Bible characters,
- setting up props for Wild Bible Adventures, and
- leading four sessions of Wild Bible Adventures each day.

JOIN THE WILD RIDE AT AVALANCHE RANCH!

Job Description

CHADDER'S WILD WEST THEATER LEADER

RELATED INTERESTS

You'll enjoy leading Chadder's Wild West Theater if you enjoy any of the following activities:

- watching movies,
- acting or drama,
- leading discussions, and
- operating electronic equipment.

QUALIFICATIONS

You'll be a successful Chadder's Wild West Theater Leader if you

- love the Lord and love children,
- have an interest in Bible study skills,
- know how to operate your church's TV and DVD player,
- enjoy facilitating group discussions, and
- ask questions to help kids connect the Bible Point they've learned in *Chadder's Wild West Adventure* to their everyday lives.

RESPONSIBILITIES

As a Chadder's Wild West Theater Leader, you'll be responsible for

- attending scheduled leader training,
- repeating the daily Bible Point as you teach,
- setting up a TV and DVD player,
- cuing *Chadder's Wild West Adventure* to each day's segment,
- helping Ranch Crew Leaders facilitate group discussions,
- handing out Bible Memory Buddies to children, and
- leading four sessions of Chadder's Wild West Theater each day.

JOIN THE WILD RIDE AT AVALANCHE RANCH!

SHOWTIME ROUNDUP LEADER

RELATED INTERESTS

You'll enjoy leading Showtime Roundup if you enjoy any of the following activities:

- public speaking,
- acting or drama,
- storytelling,
- making people laugh, and
- supervising teams of people.

QUALIFICATIONS

You'll be a successful Showtime Roundup Leader if you

- love the Lord and love children,
- enjoy being in front of people,
- are an expressive storyteller,
- like to laugh and have a good sense of humor, and
- can encourage and affirm kids' participation in each day's Showtime Roundup.

RESPONSIBILITIES

As Showtime Roundup Leader, you'll be responsible for

- attending scheduled leader training,
- repeating the daily Bible Point as you teach,
- collecting necessary supplies,
- setting up props for each day's Showtime Roundup,
- practicing each day's Showtime Roundup script ahead of time,
- recruiting and training other station leaders to assist you,
- leading Showtime Roundup for the entire Avalanche Ranch each day, and
- assisting the director as needed.

JOIN THE WILD RIDE AT AVALANCHE RANCH!

Job Description

Prairie Dog Preschool Director

Related Interests

You'll enjoy leading Prairie Dog Preschool if you enjoy any of the following activities:

- playing with young children,
- storytelling,
- singing, and
- being outdoors.

Qualifications

You'll be a successful Prairie Dog Preschool Director if you

- love the Lord and love children;
- get down on the floor and interact with children at their eye level;
- use simple language that preschoolers can understand; and
- stock your room with blocks, dress-up clothes, modeling dough, and other age-appropriate toys and supplies.

Responsibilities

As a Prairie Dog Preschool Director, you'll be responsible for

- attending scheduled leader training,
- repeating the daily Bible Point as you teach,
- collecting necessary supplies,
- leading a team of Ranch Crew Leaders for preschoolers, and
- leading a team of Prairie Dog Preschool station leaders.

JOIN THE WILD RIDE AT AVALANCHE RANCH!

Craft and Play Leader

Related Interests

You'll enjoy leading Craft and Play if you enjoy the following activities:

- watching preschoolers have a great time,
- arts and crafts, and
- working with your hands.

Qualifications

You'll be a successful Craft and Play Leader if you

- love the Lord and love children,
- are creative and fun-loving,
- can give clear directions to children, and
- show patience while working with lots of children.

Responsibilities

As a Craft and Play Leader, you'll be responsible for

- attending scheduled leader training,
- reading the Prairie Dog Preschool Craft and Play Leader Manual,
- collecting necessary supplies,
- preparing sample crafts before Avalanche Ranch,
- repeating the daily Bible Point as you teach,
- helping children create one-of-a-kind crafts,
- guiding preschoolers in easy fine-motor activities, and
- leading three sessions of Craft and Play each day.

Join the wild ride at Avalanche Ranch!

Games Leader

Related Interests

You'll enjoy leading Games if you enjoy the following activities:

- team sports,
- outdoor recreational activities, and
- encouraging others to do their best.

Qualifications

You'll be a successful Games Leader if you

- love the Lord and love children;
- enjoy playing games;
- are positive, active, and energetic; and
- can organize and motivate children.

Responsibilities

As a Prairie Dog Preschool Games Leader, you'll be responsible for

- attending scheduled leader training,
- reading the Prairie Dog Preschool Games Leader Manual,
- repeating the daily Bible Point as you teach,
- collecting necessary supplies and equipment for the games,
- clearly explaining each game, and
- leading three sessions of Games each day.

Join the wild ride at Avalanche Ranch!

Bible Adventures and Missions Leader

Related Interests

You'll enjoy leading Bible Adventures and Missions if you enjoy the following activities:

- storytelling,
- missions and outreach,
- acting or drama,
- leading discussions, and
- surprising others.

Qualifications

You'll be a successful Bible Adventures and Missions Leader if you

- love the Lord and love children;
- have a flair for drama and can play a role convincingly;
- relish a fast-paced, exciting atmosphere;
- believe in hands-on discovery as a learning technique; and
- feel comfortable facilitating group discussions.

Responsibilities

As a Bible Adventures and Missions Leader, you'll be responsible for

- attending scheduled leader training,
- reading the Prairie Dog Preschool Bible Adventures and Missions Leader Manual,
- repeating the daily Bible Point as you teach,
- collecting necessary supplies,
- setting up props for the Bible Adventures,
- helping kids carry out their Operation Kid-to-Kid mission, and
- leading three sessions of Bible Adventures and Missions each day.

Join the wild ride at Avalanche Ranch!

Chadder's Theater Leader

Related Interests

You'll enjoy leading Chadder's Theater if you enjoy the following activities:

- watching movies,
- acting or drama,
- leading discussions, and
- operating electronic equipment.

Qualifications

You'll be a successful Chadder's Theater Leader if you

- love the Lord and love children,
- know how to operate your church's TV and DVD player,
- enjoy facilitating group discussions, and
- ask questions to help kids connect the Bible Point they've learned in *Chadder's Wild West Adventure* to their everyday lives.

Responsibilities

As a Chadder's Theater Leader, you'll be responsible for

- attending scheduled leader training,
- reading the Prairie Dog Preschool Chadder's Theater Leader Manual,
- repeating the daily Bible Point as you teach,
- setting up a TV and DVD player,
- helping Ranch Crew Leaders facilitate group discussions,
- handing out Bible Memory Buddies to children, and
- leading three sessions of Chadder's Theater each day.

Join the wild ride at Avalanche Ranch!

JOIN THE AVALANCHE RANCH TEAM!

We're rounding up a herd of Ranch Crew Leaders!

QUALIFICATIONS

- Be at least 14 years old.
- Love the Lord.
- Love children.
- Like to have fun.
- Have some experience working with children.

RESPONSIBILITIES

- Attend a leader training meeting.
- Attend Avalanche Ranch each day.
- Participate in fun activities while shepherding a group of three to five elementary-age kids.
- Arrive 20 minutes early to greet crew members each day.

If you're interested, sign below or see _____ **today!**

Avalanche Ranch Director

NAME	PHONE NUMBER	E-MAIL ADDRESS
_____	_____	_____
_____	_____	_____
_____	_____	_____
_____	_____	_____
_____	_____	_____
_____	_____	_____
_____	_____	_____
_____	_____	_____
_____	_____	_____

RECRUITING RANCH CREW LEADERS FOR PRESCHOOLERS

Your youngest participants need Ranch Crew Leaders, too! Like Ranch Crew Leaders for the elementary-age kids, Ranch Crew Leaders for preschoolers don't need to prepare anything in advance. In fact, their jobs are even easier! Instead of *leading* Ranch Crews, Ranch Crew Leaders help their preschool crews follow directions given by the Prairie Dog Preschool Director.

Ranch Crew Leaders for preschoolers play with children, help them complete art projects, and keep them together when they leave the room. To ensure adequate supervision for the preschoolers who attend your Avalanche Ranch, you need one Ranch Crew Leader for every five preschool-age children.

What kind of person would make a good Ranch Crew Leader for preschoolers?

A RANCH CREW LEADER FOR PRESCHOOLERS IS

- a friend and a helper.
- someone who helps children complete activities.
- someone who gets down on the floor to interact with children.
- someone who encourages children.

Photocopy the "Howdy, Buckaroos!" handout (p. 121), and post it in your church lobby. You'll be pleasantly surprised at how many Ranch Crew Leaders for preschoolers join your team!

RECRUITING

Howdy, Buckaroos!

Join the Prairie Dog Preschool team at Avalanche Ranch VBS!

Qualifications

- Be at least 14 years old.
- Love the Lord.
- Love children.
- Like to have fun.
- Have some experience working with children.

Responsibilities

- Attend a leader training meeting.
- Attend Avalanche Ranch each day.
- Participate in fun activities while shepherding a group of three to five preschool-age children.
- Arrive 20 minutes early to greet the children in your crew.

If you're interested, sign below or see _____ today!

Prairie Dog Preschool Director

Name	Phone Number	E-mail Address
_____	_____	_____
_____	_____	_____
_____	_____	_____
_____	_____	_____
_____	_____	_____
_____	_____	_____
_____	_____	_____

RECRUITING SIGN-IN PERSONNEL AND REGISTRAR

Field Test Findings

This may seem obvious, but be sure your registration team members really do read the registration section in this Director Manual. We find that our host church directors who follow these instructions to the letter have great success.

Trail Tip

A crew of registration "experts" will make the first day feel like a breeze for everyone else. We highly recommend recruiting a small crew of volunteers devoted to registration. You'll love handing that responsibility over to someone else, freeing you up to attend to other details. Teamwork is the way to go!

Trail Tip

You might consider enlisting a few middle schoolers to act as guides who will lead children inside and help them find their Ranch Crews. This simple step will speak *volumes* to parents (and kids) who are new to the church. It's a great way to get everyone off to a good start...and a wonderful way to give responsibility to middle schoolers!

It's important to have staff near the registration tables to greet, welcome, and direct children. You'll also need at least one official registrar to make sure registration goes smoothly.

For your registrar, look for someone who

- pays close attention to details,
- is organized,
- is familiar with many kids in your church (this helps when forming Ranch Crews and provides kids with a familiar face on Day 1),
- will follow registration information in this Director Manual,
- understands the "combined-age" concept, and
- meets deadlines with a cheerful spirit.

Allow the registrar to read through the registration section on page 153 of this Avalanche Ranch Director Manual several weeks before Avalanche Ranch begins. Be sure that all registration forms and phone registrations are given to the registrar.

For sign-in volunteers, look for individuals who

- are friendly and outgoing,
- are comfortable interacting with children, and
- want to help with Avalanche Ranch but can't commit much time.

You can have different sign-in greeters each day—kids will love the surprise! Encourage your greeters to dress up in Avalanche Ranch staff T-shirts or Avalanche Ranch–theme clothes. Greeters can direct children to Prairie Dog Preschool or help kids find their Ranch Crew Leaders. We've even heard from churches that recruited volunteers to say goodbye to the kids as they left each day! Wow! What an awesome way to affirm and bless each child!

RECRUITING

FILLING OUT YOUR STAFF

In addition to station leaders, Ranch Crew Leaders and registration staff, you may want to enlist the following staff members:

■ **co-director or Crew Leader Director**—Pulling off a successful VBS takes a lot of attention to detail. That's why you'll benefit from another creative brain and an additional set of helping hands. A Crew Leader Director is responsible for training, communicating with, and checking in with each Ranch Crew Leader daily during Avalanche Ranch. Handing this responsibility off to one person is a great way to see that it's done well!

■ **publicity coordinator**—This person is responsible for coordinating publicity before and during your Avalanche Ranch. This might include selecting publicity supplies, planning outreach publicity campaigns, inviting local TV or newspaper reporters, contacting church and community members, or arranging for community news releases. (TV coverage on Day 5 would be a super way to tell your community about Operation Kid-to-Kid!) The publicity section of this manual will help your publicity coordinator plan a great publicity campaign using the Avalanche Ranch publicity supplies available from Group Publishing and your local Group supplier.

■ **decoration coordinator**—Planning and making decorations can be time consuming. Find someone with a creative, artistic flair who can highlight your theme, and then hand off the decorating booklet found in your Starter Kit. (Be sure to send your decoration coordinator to www.groupoutlet.com for hot decorations at cool prices!)

■ **family resource coordinator**—This person is responsible for collecting the completed order forms and money for family resources (such as *Sing & Play Stampede Music* audiocassettes or CDs or *Chadder's Wild West Adventure* videos or DVDs), placing the order, and then distributing the items when they arrive. You may want to direct this person to the "Follow-Up" section of this manual (pp. 189-197).

■ **transportation coordinator**—This person is responsible for coordinating transportation to and from Avalanche Ranch. This might include organizing car pools, planning van or bus routes, or actually picking up children and transporting them to your facility.

■ **child care coordinator**—This person is responsible for providing or coordinating child care for the Avalanche Ranch staff. If possible, child care should be provided for all children (age 3 and younger) of station leaders and Ranch Crew Leaders. You may even want to provide this staff member with the Little Buckaroos: Infants, Toddlers, and Twos program so *everyone* can crawl into big Bible adventures! Or provide an entire program for the littlest participants! Invite all new parents to bring their wee ones!

Trail Tip We've received many letters from VBS directors who entered a VBS float in a local parade. Consider creating a float that's decorated as an Avalanche Ranch celebration. Have kids and adults decked out in costumes! Or let kids toss Bible Memory Buddies into the crowd. Blast Sing & Play Stampede music as you "float" by. What a fun way to alert the community about your Avalanche Ranch!

- **extra registration workers**—You'll need a team of four to five registration workers to ensure smooth, speedy check-in on Day 1. Registration workers check in kids who have preregistered and make sure walk-in participants complete registration forms. With your guidance, registration workers also assign walk-in participants to Ranch Crews. Plan to meet with the registration team *before* registration to go over the registration information on pages 153-174.

- **music accompanist**—If you want to use live music during Sing & Play Stampede, enlist a pianist, guitarist, drummer, or even an entire Avalanche Ranch band to help lead singing. Some churches have pulled together a VBS praise band, composed of high schoolers! (Have your accompanist listen to the *Sing & Play Stampede Music* CD or audiocassette to hear the speed and beat of the music that worked so well in our field test.) Remind your music makers to learn the new VBS music that's especially designed to reinforce the theme and Bible Point each day.

- **VBS fundraiser champion**—Hand over the new Fund-Your-VBS Kit, and let someone focus on energizing your whole congregation. This all-inclusive kit makes it easy to raise money—and enthusiasm—for your Avalanche Ranch!

WHEN YOUR STAFF IS COMPLETE, YOU'RE READY TO CELEBRATE AT YOUR AVALANCHE RANCH!

Staff Training for Avalanche Ranch

Use these ideas to train the whole pack!

USING THE *WAH-HOO!* DVD

We know *you're* excited about Avalanche Ranch. The *Wah-hoo!* DVD can help you get others in your church excited, too. The DVD is divided into the following segments: recruiting, overview, Operation Kid-to-Kid, and pass-along training.

The *Wah-hoo!* DVD really does make your job easy. Your staff will love seeing a real Avalanche Ranch in progress, and they'll be reassured that their activities really *will* be a success. This is a simple way to recruit, train, and prepare your staff.

■ **The recruiting section** makes it easy to get all your Avalanche Ranch volunteers! This section contains three short "commercials" that you can show before adult Sunday school classes, during announcement time at worship services, or any time people are gathered. You might even set up a TV and DVD player near your volunteer sign-in area and leave these commercials playing. With these additional recruiting tools, you'll look like a pro!

■ **The overview segment** gives a brief introduction to Group's Avalanche Ranch. In this two-minute segment, you'll discover what makes Avalanche Ranch different from other programs. Your church leaders, your Christian education board, and your congregation will see that this VBS program results in deeper Bible learning, not just games and crafts. Show the clip in your children's church or Sunday school classes to get kids excited about discovering God's love. (This is a great way to get most of your kids preregistered, too.) This short "teaser" will get everyone geared up for your exciting adventure!

By the way, did you realize that we test ideas that never make it to you? Thanks to input from VBS directors from across North America (and beyond!), every aspect of the Avalanche Ranch program is tested. We listen and make changes. If something flops in the field test, we try again—and test again! We make mistakes so you don't have to!

■ **The Operation Kid-to-Kid segment** will get everyone wild about this world-changing missions project. All churches that participate in an Avalanche Ranch VBS will join together to share God's love with orphans in Africa! Use this clip to explain the missions project and help everyone catch the vision.

- **The pass-along training portion** will get your entire staff ready for action. DVD segments include topics such as...

  - A Day at Avalanche Ranch
  - Decorating Tips
  - Networking
  - Prairie Dog Preschool
  - Teaching Tips for Station Leaders and Crew Leaders
  - Treasure Verse Actions
  - The Daily Challenge
  - Working With Combined-Ages

In these training segments, station leaders will see kids successfully completing the activities described in their leader manuals. Crew leaders will get to peek at great crew leaders. Your staff will see kids in a real Avalanche Ranch program enjoying Horseplay Games, serving and tasting Chuck Wagon Chow, creating spectacular Bible Point Crafts, and discovering Bible truths in new and meaningful ways.

Through interviews with real staff members from our field test, your volunteers can learn how to work with their Ranch Crews, discover what's expected of them, and see the impact they can have on the kids at Avalanche Ranch.

STAFF TRAINING MEETING

Trail Tip
Your Sing & Play Stampede Leader will need a set of Bible Point posters to use every day. You can use the same set for this training meeting.

Trail Tip
The *Sing & Play Stampede Music* DVD lets volunteers see Sing & Play Stampede fun in action. This DVD is a super way to add enthusiasm, build confidence, and teach all 10 Avalanche Ranch songs. Use the kids on the video to teach *your* kids!

You'll need the following supplies:

- CD player
- name tags*
- TV and DVD player
- markers
- tape
- paint markers

GAME SUPPLIES

- chairs (1 per staff member)

SNACK SUPPLIES

- 1 graham cracker per participant
- ½ chocolate candy bar (such as Hershey's) per participant
- 2 cans of vanilla frosting per Ranch Crew in Snacks Service
- 2 resealable sandwich bags per Ranch Crew in Snacks Service
- 2 plastic knives per Ranch Crew in Snacks Service
- 1 small paper plate per participant
- 1 cup per participant
- 1 napkin per participant
- pitchers of water or juice
- hand wipes

ADDITIONAL SUPPLIES

- Daily Challenge Wow Cows*
- sample Operation Kid-to-Kid Prayer Bear
- *Clip Art, Song Lyrics, and Decorating* CD*
- Wrangler Ringers* or other attention-getting signals
- Avalanche Ranch staff T-shirts* (optional)

- crew leader cowboy hats** (optional)
- photocopies of the "For Ranch Crew Leaders Only" handouts (pp. 139-142) and "For Preschool Ranch Crew Leaders Only" handouts (pp. 143-144)
- Bible Point posters*
- Treasure Verse posters*
- colorful poster board (1 large sheet per Ranch Crew Leader)
- pair of scissors per Ranch Crew Leader
- 5 sheets of white poster board or foam core (for backing the Bible Point posters)
- Crew Leader Pocket Guides*
- sample daily schedules
- map of station locations
- complete list of names and phone numbers of crew leaders, station leaders, registration staff and the VBS directors

THINGS YOU'LL FIND IN YOUR STARTER KIT:

- *Sing & Play Stampede Music* CD
- sample Wild Ride Bible Guide
- *Wah-hoo!* DVD
- Avalanche Ranch leader manuals
- *Sing & Play Stampede Music* DVD* (optional)

*These items are available from Group Publishing and your local Group supplier.
**available at www.groupoutlet.com

"GETTING READY"

Before the meeting, set up a TV and a DVD player in your meeting room. Insert the *Wah-hoo!* DVD. Set chairs facing the TV.

Decorate your meeting room to look like you're at Avalanche Ranch. Set up the Avalanche Ranch display near your entryway, hang a herd of inflatable cows from the ceiling, drape bandannas over tables or chairs, set up a few imitation Christmas trees, and hang up the Treasure Verse posters.

Provide a Crew Leader Pocket Guide for each Ranch Crew Leader. (Crew Leader Pocket Guides for elementary *and* preschool crew leaders are available from Group Publishing or your Group supplier.) Or create an informative "Trail Tips" packet for each Ranch Crew Leader to keep. Include the following:

- photocopies of the "For Ranch Crew Leaders Only" handouts (pp. 139-142)

- sample daily schedule (p. 85)

- list of station leader names (p. 101)

- age-level information sheets (on page 31 of this manual and page 19 of the Prairie Dog Preschool Director Manual)

- "Helping Children Follow Jesus" handout (p. 181)

Distribute the Pocket Guides (or packets) to your Ranch Crew Leaders as they enter the room.

Set out the snack-making supplies on one or two tables. (You'll need one snack-making table for every 10 volunteers.) Set a sheet of colorful poster board and a pair of scissors under each chair. Place name tags and markers near your entryway. Tape each Bible Point poster to a sheet of white poster board or foam core. (This makes posters stiff so they're easier to hold up for your staff to see.) Place a roll of tape and the posters where you can reach them easily.

Play the *Sing & Play Stampede Music* CD as volunteers arrive. (This sets the mood and gives everyone a chance to preview the awesome music they'll be hearing all week.) Greet each Ranch Crew Leader or Ranch Station Leader with a warm smile. Encourage each volunteer to write his or her name on a name tag. Then ask your staff members to sit down. Be sure to thank everyone for coming to this meeting and for helping with Avalanche Ranch.

Trail Tip Crew Leader Pocket Guides not only save you time and energy but also include daily discussion questions so leaders can be better prepared. Your crew leaders will appreciate such a practical, handy guidebook!

Trail Tip The information contained in the Crew Leader Pocket Guide and "For Ranch Crew Leaders Only" handouts will be incredibly helpful to your staff. Be sure to provide this information and stress the importance of reading them *before* Avalanche Ranch begins. Ranch Crew Leaders will likely find that many of their questions are answered here.

Let's get started!

"WELCOME"

When everyone has arrived, gradually turn down the volume on the CD player, and then stop the music. Sound the Wrangler Ringer, or use another attention-getting signal. Say: **Howdy! My name is** [name], **and I'll be your Avalanche Ranch Director. It's great to have each one of you on our Avalanche Ranch staff.**

My goal is to give you a taste of what's going to happen at Avalanche Ranch. You'll leave here prepared to be the best staff ever. First, we'll spend some time focusing on the kids who will attend Avalanche Ranch. After all, those kids are the entire reason for the program! We'll have fun with some activities and discuss your roles at VBS. Then I'll give you some helpful tips to make you the best crew leaders and station leaders around. Let's start our training time with a prayer.

Pray: **Dear God, thank you for allowing us to serve you with VBS. Thank you for each person here and for the gifts and abilities he or she brings to our children. Be with us as we prepare our hearts and minds for an important week, where kids will grow in their friendship with your Son, Jesus. Guide our time together. In Jesus' name, amen.**

ANIMAL ANTICS

Say: **At Avalanche Ranch, kids will head to a high-mountain ranch filled with bucking broncos, soaring eagles, and friendly cattle dogs. Let's see what happens during a day at Avalanche Ranch VBS.**

Play the "A Day at Avalanche Ranch" segment of the *Wahhoo!* DVD. Then say: **Most of us have been to some kind of ranch—or maybe the closest *you've* been to a ranch is eating barbecue. Find a couple of friends sitting nearby, and let each person tell about a time you went west or spent time at a ranch. Maybe it was your eighth birthday party and you had a western-themed party. Or maybe you went on a trail ride at camp. I'll give you about five minutes to share.**

Play "The Great Adventure" while staff members share. When the song ends, turn off the CD player, and sound the Wrangler Ringer.

Say: **This is my Wrangler Ringer. I'll use it whenever I need to get your attention. At Avalanche Ranch we'll use attention-getting signals to let kids and crew leaders know when it's time to stop talking and pay attention. I'll also use the Wrangler Ringer each day at Avalanche Ranch to let you know when it's time to send kids to their next stations. Station leaders, you may want to use your own Wrangler Ringer during Avalanche Ranch. It's a lot easier and nicer than lots of "shushing." Each day is filled with activities, so**

you won't want to lose a minute. Now let's hear from a few of you cowpokes. Call on a few people to share. Then say: **Turn to a friend and discuss this question:**

■ **Why might *this* VBS experience be memorable for the kids who attend?** (They'll have fun; they'll make new friends; they'll learn something new about Jesus.)

 Play "God Is Good (All the Time)" while partners share. When the song ends, turn off the CD.

Say: **You'll find that we use pair-shares and group discussions a lot at Avalanche Ranch. That gives everyone, even shy or quiet kids, a chance to talk. Another way to get everyone involved is through crew roles. Each day when kids come to Avalanche Ranch, they'll choose one of five roles in the crew. Kids can choose to be Readers, Prayer People, Ranch Guides, Coaches, or Materials Managers. Now I'd like to hear some of the things you talked about.**

Let a few people share what they discussed.

Reader

Coach

Materials Manager

Ranch Guide

Prayer Person

Trail Tip
If you're providing attention-getting signals for your station leaders, this would be a good time to distribute them. You can use the Wrangler Ringer, available from Group Publishing and your Group supplier, or any other noisemakers of your choice.

TRAINING

WAH-HOO!

Say: **We want this to be a memorable experience for kids because they'll grow in their love for and understanding of God. One way we do that is through the Bible Point.**

Each day at Avalanche Ranch, kids will discover one important truth about God. We call this the Bible Point. Station leaders, you'll say the Point many times each day. That's because repetition is an important way for kids to learn. Crew leaders, you'll join your kids in shouting "Wah-hoo!" each time you hear the Point. You'll also make a sign for "Wah-hoo!" It goes like this. Demonstrate the lasso-twirling motion, according to the margin illustration.

At Avalanche Ranch, we want kids to discover new and exciting things about God. Find three people, and form a small group. When your group is together, quickly brainstorm some things that are important in the lives of kids today. What do they talk about when parents aren't listening? You'll have about one minute to think of as many things as you can. I'll sound the Wrangler Ringer when it's time to stop.

 Play "Worship You Forever" while groups are working. After one minute, sound the Wrangler Ringer to call time. Let each group share a few of its ideas aloud.

Say: **Kids are excited about so many things today—clothes, toys, video games, movies—that it's hard to keep up. But at Avalanche Ranch, we want kids to be excited about God. One way to reach into the hearts and minds of kids is through relationships. That's why at Avalanche Ranch, kids will form small mixed-age groups called Ranch Crews. Let's take a quick peek at some tips on working with mixed-age crews.**

Play the "Working With Mixed-Age Crews" segment of the *Wah-hoo!* DVD.

Say: **Ranch Crews are a great way for kids to build and nurture friendships as they learn. Right now we're going to make a sign for each Ranch Crew, where those friendships will grow. These signs will help kids find their crews each day.**

Lead the group in counting off to assign crew numbers, and then give Ranch Crew Leaders five minutes to write their numbers as large as possible on the sheets of poster board under their chairs.

Field Test Findings We had many crews that grew to more than five kids during the week, making it a challenge for crew leaders (and station leaders). Let *everyone* succeed at Avalanche Ranch! Be sure to let your crew leaders know that their crews should consist of only up to five children. If the crew grows, staff members should alert the VBS director so he or she can move children into smaller crews or form new crews.

Field Test Findings We discovered that it's crucial to get your staff prepared to work with mixed-age groups of kids. Crew leaders who approached the multi-age concept with a positive, can-do attitude had a wonderful experience. (Many were secretly surprised that it worked as well as it did!) They were better prepared to help kids work as a team or family.

If your entire staff made it to the meeting, pat yourself on the back. Now you have extra hands to create the preschool signs. Preschoolers join crews that have colorful creature names rather than numbers—Red Ponies, Brown Boots, Blue Bison, or Yellow Stars, for example.

RED PONIES

Encourage them to add Avalanche Ranch–theme shapes, such as horses, mountains, pine trees, or horseshoes. Station leaders may want to work on decorating their door signs during this time.

After five minutes, sound the Wrangler Ringer to regain everyone's attention. Say: **Each crew sign represents about five children who will discover more about God's love at Avalanche Ranch. Gather with a few people nearby—people you haven't worked with yet—and form a circle. Put your signs in the middle of your circle, and pray for the kids who will be in those crews.**

Allow about two minutes for groups to gather and pray. Then say: **Amen. Have one of your group members bring your stack of signs up front while the rest of you return to your seats.**

OVERVIEW

When volunteers have returned to their seats, say: **Now let's explore** *your* **roles at Avalanche Ranch. Whatever your role here, you'll work with kids who are in crews. To help you be the wildest leaders in town, let's get an overview of what you can expect during Avalanche Ranch.**

 Start the DVD, and show the overview segment. When that segment ends, stop the DVD, and answer any questions about the overall format. You may want to refer staff members to the sample schedules in the packets you assembled. (This visual usually helps people grasp the rotation concept.)

Say: **Now check out these tips for being the best staff around.** Play the "Teaching Tips for Station Leaders and Crew Leaders" segment of the DVD. When the segment ends, continue: **Let's dig deeper into these training tips. Each day at Avalanche Ranch, kids will meet a Bible Memory Buddy who reminds them of the daily Bible Point and Treasure Verse. You'll get a special sneak peek at the Bible Memory Buddies because they're going to help me with training today!**

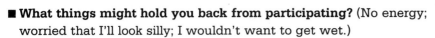

PARTICIPATE

> **Jump into Avalanche Ranch and get involved!**

Hold up the poster of Buc, and say: **This is Buc, our bucking bronco! He's here to remind you to jump in and participate.** Ask:

■ **What things might hold you back from participating?** (No energy; worried that I'll look silly; I wouldn't want to get wet.)

■ **Why do you think it's important to get involved?** (So kids will see that it's fun; to encourage kids to participate; to get to know kids; to have fun.)

Say: **One great thing about Avalanche Ranch is that it gives you the opportunity to be a kid again. So we expect you to jump in with a big smile! You can practice with this game!**

Have staff members move their chairs into a large circle, facing in. Choose one person to stand in the middle of the circle, while everyone else sits.

Point out that there's only one chair open. The person in the middle is going to try to sit in the open chair. The only way that person can be stopped from sitting in the chair is for the person sitting to the left of that chair to move into it. Demonstrate by having the person sitting next to the open chair move into that seat.

Then indicate the new empty chair, and explain that the person in the middle will keep trying to get to the next empty chair as everyone in the circle keeps on scooting over, so they will have to scoot over quickly! Say: **When the person in the middle gets to the empty chair, I'll choose someone else to have a turn.**

Play for about five minutes, giving several staff members a chance to be in the middle. Then form small-group circles for discussion. Ask:

■ **What was special about the open chair?** (It was the only one; everyone wanted to get to it.)

■ **What's special about God?** (He's real; he's the only one; he can do anything.)

Say: **Our Treasure Verse on Day 1 is Jeremiah 10:10: "The Lord is the only true God."**

The chair in this game was special because it was the only one. God is special, too, because GOD IS REAL. He's our one God. We worship God because he's our only one real God!

Sound the Wrangler Ringer, and then say: **Your wholehearted, joyful participation in every activity will say so much to the kids who attend our Avalanche Ranch. Kids who are shy, quiet, or think they're too cool for church will let down *their* guard and get involved, too.**

Have staff members move their chairs back into the original formation so they can see you.

Trail Tip

After playing this game, you may want to explain why the games at Avalanche Ranch are cooperative, not competitive. Point out how much fun it is when everyone succeeds. Encourage your staff members to encourage cooperation in every facet of your program.

FOLLOW DIRECTIONS

Stick to the directions!

Say: **Let's see what our next Bible Memory Buddy can tell us.**

Hold up the poster of Boss, and say: **This is Boss the longhorn steer. His long, pointed horns remind us to stick to the directions! Station leaders, the activities in your manuals have been tested, tweaked, and retested, so be sure to follow them as closely as possible. Crew leaders, you need to listen to the station leaders and follow *their* instructions.**

At Avalanche Ranch, we're all a team—crew leaders helping station leaders and vice versa. Even though crew leaders won't prepare anything, they have the great responsibility of making sure kids get the most out of every station. Following directions is a lot like following a recipe. I'll give you some practice as we test one of our Avalanche Ranch snacks!

Demonstrate how to make Stick With You S'Mores, using the following instructions. Then form groups of five, and let each group

make snacks for about 10 minutes. Play the *Sing & Play Stampede Music* CD while participants work.

1. Break each graham cracker in half.

2. Use a "pastry bag" to squeeze frosting onto the graham crackers.

3. Use a plastic knife to spread the frosting over each graham cracker.

4. Add half of a chocolate candy bar on one graham cracker.

5. Place the second graham cracker on top for a finished s'more.

Encourage staff members to each take a snack and enjoy it while you continue the training session. Ask:

■ **What do you hope "sticks with" kids when they leave Avalanche Ranch?** (What they learn about Jesus; their friendships; that church is a fun place; the Bible stories.)

Say: **Let's see if we have another Buddy to help us become the best team around.**

CIRCLE UP FOR DISCUSSION

Hold up the poster of Ranger, and say: **This is Ranger the bison. Ranger reminds us to circle up for discussions so we can see everyone in the herd. You might be tempted to let your crew lean against a wall or lie around during discussion times. After all, you and the kids are going to get tired. Let's see what that's like.**

Circle up so you can see everyone in the herd!

Form groups of five. Direct small groups to move their chairs into a line (if the chairs aren't already in a line), so staff members are side-by-side, as they discuss the following question:

■ **Tell about a treasured stuffed animal or toy you had as a child.**

 Play "Awesome God" while crews discuss the question. When the song ends, sound the Wrangler Ringer.

Say: **Now we'll see how discussion circles work. But first, let's take a quick peek at an important missions project we'll participate in.**

 Show the "Operation Kid-to-Kid" segment from the DVD. When the segment ends, turn off the DVD player and ask each small group to form a little circle. (We call these "knee-to-knee" circles because kids are most often sitting cross-legged on the floor, and their knees should be right next to the friends sitting on either side.) Allow group members to discuss the following question:

■ **Why do you think Operation Kid-to-Kid will be meaningful to the kids in our church?** (It's about stuffed animals; kids like to have stuffed animals; kids will like to give something they've actually made.)

Play "Praise the Lord" (Psalm 150:6) while crews discuss. When the song ends, turn off the CD and sound the Wrangler Ringer. Ask:

■ **What differences did you notice in your two discussions?** (It was hard to hear when we were in a line; I listened to other conversations the first time; we were all really tuned in the second time.)

Trail Tip

It's a good idea to give Ranch Crew Leaders some idea as to what they can expect at Avalanche Ranch. After all, this isn't the VBS that many of us grew up with! Let crew leaders know that a little extra noise and movement is OK—that's how kids learn and explore awesome Bible truths. Remind them that even though kids aren't sitting in quiet rows with their hands folded, kids will be taking God's Word to heart.

Say: **God can allow priceless conversation and discovery to take place within crew circles! Discussion circles are important because they help kids focus *in* on what's being said, while they allow crew leaders to make excellent eye contact. Station leaders, remember to wait until all crews are circled up before starting your discussion time.**

Crew leaders, some station leaders may ask you to actually ask the questions, which are found in your Crew Leader Pocket Guides. Hold up a sample Crew Leader Pocket Guide. **It's important that you refer to the questions and make sure each child has the chance to answer them.**

THE DAILY CHALLENGE

Hold up the poster of Skye, and say: **This is Skye, the majestic eagle. Skye reminds us to keep an eagle eye open for kids living out what they're learning. That's the Daily Challenge.**

Show the "Daily Challenge" section of the DVD.

Open up a Wild Ride Bible Guide, and hold up a Daily Challenge. Say: **Crew leaders, as you sit with your crews and eat Chuck Wagon Chow, kids will open up their Wild Ride Bible Guides and look at that day's Daily Challenge. Be sure to read each challenge aloud so kids understand what the challenges are.** Read some of the challenges from the Wild Ride Bible Guide. **Then help children *each* choose the challenge they'll do when they go home and mark it with a Wow**

Use your eagle-eyes to watch kids living out God's Word!

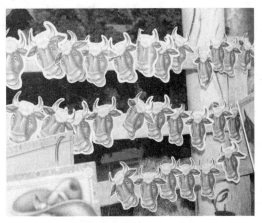

Cow sticker from their student book. Talk about what it will be like. Will people be surprised? What will it feel like? How will you remember to do it?

At the end of the day, the Showtime Roundup Leader will remind kids to do their Daily Challenge. Crew leaders will help kids tear out that day's challenge, wrap them around their wrists, and fasten them with Avalanche Ranch stickers—these will be in each Wild Ride Bible Guide. That way, kids will wear their challenges home! Preschoolers won't wear their Daily Challenges home, but the preschool Daily Challenges are on the back of their Bible Activity Pages, which go home every day. Preschool crew leaders, be sure to take time throughout each day to talk about the Daily Challenges. Even little preschoolers can share God's love in big ways!

The next day, during Sing & Play Stampede, the Sing & Play Stampede Leader will give you a special time to share about yesterday's Daily Challenges. *Remember, this isn't something you'll reward kids for or bribe them to do!* Please don't offer stickers or toys or prizes for doing the Daily Challenge. We want kids to share God's love just because it's so fun to do! As kids share about how they carried out the Daily Challenge, crew leaders will take a special Daily Challenge Wow Cow from their Crew Bags. Hold up a Wow Cow.

When the Sing & Play Stampede Leader gives the signal, you'll hang that day's Wow Cow on the fence of the corral in the front of the room. Explain what your Daily Challenge Corral will be like and how you expect crew leaders to hang the cows on the fence.

At the end of our Avalanche Ranch, the corral will be filled with colorful reminders of God's love!

Answer any questions volunteers might have about the Daily Challenge before moving to the next section.

Field Test Findings

The Daily Challenge is an important part of Avalanche Ranch. Our staff *loved* hearing how kids had lived out the Bible Point at home each day. Some were acts of service, such as helping make dinner or cleaning a sibling's room. Other kids chose to pray with station leaders before Avalanche Ranch. We even heard of kids who stood up to a bully at sports practice. Celebrate all the ways kids can show their love for God!

Field Test Findings

We can't say it enough—please don't turn the Daily Challenge into something kids do to earn prizes. At our field test, we intentionally kept bribery and rewards completely out of the picture...and kids were incredibly excited about the Daily Challenge! Yes, they did the challenges *without* external incentives—it was purely from the heart. Help kids develop a heart for sharing Jesus' love in tangible ways, purely for the joy of serving.

SHOW GOD'S LOVE

Be a friend!

Hold up the poster of Shadow, and say: **Finally, I want you to meet Shadow the friendly cattle dog. She'll encourage us to be a friend in all we do. By taking the time to staff our Avalanche Ranch, you're sharing Jesus' love with the children who will come to our VBS! To be sure we're following Jesus' example, ask yourself this question every day: Would Jesus treat a child this way?**

Let's close in a special prayer. Stand and join hands. Pause while staff members follow your instructions. **I'll start the prayer and ask God to help our VBS be…and then I'll pause. Let's go around the circle and each person say one word. Say a word that tells how you want your crew to be—warm, inviting, or maybe safe. Or say a word that describes how you want your station to be for kids— exciting, surprising, or joyful. Then I'll close.**

Pray: **Heavenly Father, thank you that we get the privilege of serving you at Avalanche Ranch. Thank you for each person here, their love for children, and their passion for you. We give this VBS to you. We pray that, with your help, our VBS will be…**

When each person has said one word, close by saying: **In Jesus' name, amen.**

While your team is assembled, it's a good idea to take care of lots of "housekeeping" items. You might want to use the clip art on the *Clip Art, Song Lyrics, and Decorating* CD to create an "Avalanche Ranch Basics" handout. Be sure to include the following:

- Tell your staff what time to arrive on the first day and where to meet. If you're planning to have staff devotions, let your staff know so they can arrive early. Be sure they know meeting times and places each day after that as well.

- Hand out a copy of a sample daily schedule so all staff can get a good understanding of how a day at Avalanche Ranch will work.

- Distribute a map that shows where each station will be located.

- Give a complete list of names and phone numbers of crew leaders, station leaders, registration staff, and the VBS director(s).

- Inform station leaders and crew leaders of procedures you'll follow if there's a fire or another emergency.

WHAT'S A RANCH CREW LEADER?

If you've been asked to be a Ranch Crew Leader, you've met two important qualifications: You love the Lord, and you love kids.

During Avalanche Ranch, you'll visit different stations with a group of three to five kids. **You're not in charge of preparing or teaching activities; you just get to be there and help kids enjoy them as you shepherd the members of your Ranch Crew.**

The following guidelines will help you be an awesome Ranch Crew Leader.

A RANCH CREW LEADER IS

- a friend and a helper.
- someone who knows and calls kids by name.
- someone who offers kids choices.
- someone who asks questions.
- someone who encourages kids.
- someone who supports station leaders.

WHEN TALKING WITH KIDS, SAY,

- Let's keep moving so we can do as many fun activities as possible.
- Listen carefully so you'll know what to do next.
- Stay with the Ranch Crew; we need your help in this activity!
- That's a unique way of doing things! How did you think of that? Let's try it this way.
- It's important that we all follow the instructions and work together as a team.
- Please move over here so you can see better.
- Let's all sit in a circle so we can see and hear one another better.
- Those crafts and Buddies sure are cool! Let's keep them put away so we can hear about this next activity.

DON'T SAY,

- Stop talking and get back to work.
- Be quiet and listen!
- Don't run around the room.
- You're doing it wrong!
- Don't do that!
- Stay out of that area!

For Ranch Crew Leaders Only

Most of the time, things will go smoothly for your crew, but every once in a while, you may run into a dilemma. Here's some advice on how to handle different challenges.

IF MY CREW WON'T STAY TOGETHER

Encourage your Ranch Guide to come up with creative ways to travel. Or work with your Coach to come up with cheers to say as you travel.

IF OLDER KIDS ARE UNHAPPY BEING GROUPED WITH MIXED AGES

Highlight their helping role. Encourage them to help younger kids with crafts and other activities. Acknowledge them by telling younger kids, "[Name of older child] is really good at that. Why don't you ask him [or her] to help?"

IF I HAVE A CLIQUE IN MY CREW

Cliques can make the Ranch Crew experience unhappy for the outsiders. Encourage friendships among all crew members by pairing kids with partners they don't know very well during games and crafts.

IF A CREW MEMBER WON'T PARTICIPATE

Help shy children feel welcome by calling them by name and asking them questions directly. Respond to their questions with a smile and a statement such as "That's really interesting!" Also try giving children special jobs. For example, assign them the task of finding a place for your crew to sit at each station.

If someone doesn't want to participate in Horseplay Games, that's OK. Avalanche Ranch can be tiring! Let children rest until they're ready to participate.

IF PEOPLE IN MY CREW DON'T GET ALONG

Quietly take the children aside. Tell them you've noticed that they're not getting along. Let them know that although they don't have to be best friends, they do have to be together all week, so things will be a lot more fun if they can at least be kind to one another. (Use the daily Bible Points for these teachable moments!)

IF I HAVE AN OVERLY ACTIVE CHILD

Pair this child with yourself during partner activities, and suggest that he or she sit with you during quiet times. Try to make sitting still a game by saying, "Let's see how long you can sit still without interrupting. I'm timing you. Ready? Go!"

If the child is really uncontrollable, ask your director if you could have an Assistant Ranch Crew Leader to help.

IF MY CREW GETS TOO BIG

Avalanche Ranch is a blast, so it's likely that kids will want to bring friends. However, the activities at Avalanche Ranch are designed to work with a mixed-age crew of *no more* than five kids. If you have a small crew, you'll welcome a few additional friends into your crew family. But if your crew grows past five children, talk with your Avalanche Ranch Director as soon as possible. He or she will need to form a new crew so kids can have the best experience possible.

WHO'S WHO IN THE RANCH CREW?

During their first Sing & Play Stampede session, kids will choose Ranch Crew jobs. Each child will have one of the jobs listed in the chart below.

If your crew has fewer than five kids, some kids may have more than one job.

If children can't agree on who should perform each job, tell them that everyone will get a chance to do all the jobs. Assign kids jobs for Day 1; then rotate jobs each day so that by the end of the week, all children in the crew have had an opportunity to do each job.

Kids are excited about having special jobs. Encourage them to fulfill their roles, and provide lots of opportunities for them to do so.

JOBS	DUTIES
READER	■ likes to read ■ reads Bible passages aloud
RANCH GUIDE	■ chooses action ideas for traveling between stations (such as tiptoeing, hopping, galloping, or marching) ■ serves as line leader to guide crew through daily schedule
MATERIALS MANAGER	■ likes to distribute and collect supplies ■ carries Ranch Crew Bag ■ distributes and collects Bible Point Craft materials ■ distributes Wild Ride Bible Guides
COACH	■ likes to smile and make people happy ■ makes sure people use kind words and actions ■ leads group in cheering during Horseplay Games
PRAYER PERSON	■ likes to pray and isn't afraid to pray aloud ■ makes sure the group takes time to pray each day ■ leads or opens prayer times

For Ranch Crew Leaders Only

WHAT DO I DO AT EACH STATION?

Sing & Play Stampede is where kids worship by singing upbeat action songs. Your job at Sing & Play Stampede is to

- arrive a few minutes early,
- greet your crew members in your designated seating area,
- follow the motions and sing out loud,
- listen to how kids carried out their Daily Challenges (and share how you carried them out, too!),
- place Daily Challenge Wow Cows on the Daily Challenge Corral, and
- remember that if you get involved, the kids will, too!

Wild Bible Adventures is where kids experience the Bible story. Your job at Wild Bible Adventures is to

- line up with your crew outside the door,
- listen carefully to hear how crew leaders should help out that day,
- keep your crew together until you receive other directions, and
- encourage crew members to participate.

Cowpoke Crafts and Missions is where kids make Bible Point Crafts and talk about Operation Kid-to-Kid. Your job at Cowpoke Crafts is to

- listen carefully to the instructions because you will most likely need to repeat them for some members of your crew,
- help kids make their crafts (*when* they need help),
- ask the daily questions you've been given as kids work, and
- help clean up your area before leaving.

Horseplay Games is where kids play team-building games. Your job at Horseplay Games is to

- listen carefully to the instructions so you can help your crew members follow them,
- perform any tasks the games leader assigns to you, and
- participate in each activity and cheer on your crew members as they participate.

Surprise!
One day, your crew will arrive at Horseplay Games to discover that you're starring in that day's Spotlight Drama! Spotlight Drama is a customized slide show, featuring the kids and leaders at Avalanche Ranch. So smile! Join in the fun and be prepared to see yourself on the big screen!

Chuck Wagon Chow is where crews come for a tasty snack. (One day of VBS, your crew will help make Chuck Wagon Chow for the entire VBS!) Your job at Chuck Wagon Chow is to

- gather your crew in a designated area,
- quiet kids and help them focus on the Chuck Wagon Chow Leader as he or she explains the snack,
- help kids choose and circle their Daily Challenge, and
- help kids clean up your area before leaving.

Chadder's Wild West Theater is where children watch the *Chadder's Wild West Adventure* video. Kids also receive special Bible Memory Buddies to place in their Buddy Bags each day. Your job at Chadder's Wild West Theater is to

- encourage kids to sit still and watch the video,
- lead your crew in participating in the activities before and after the video,
- lead kids in discussion when it's called for, and
- distribute Bible Memory Buddies in a meaningful and memorable fashion.

Showtime Roundup is an exciting review of the day's lesson. Your role at Showtime Roundup is to

- lead kids to your assigned seating area,
- participate in singing and other activities,
- remind your crew to participate without being rowdy or disruptive,
- distribute Daily Challenges and help kids wrap and tape them around their wrists,
- make sure each child leaves with his or her craft, and
- collect kids' name badges and Buddy Bags as they leave and store them in your Crew Bag.

What's a Ranch Crew Leader?

If you've been asked to be a Ranch Crew Leader for preschoolers, you've met two important qualifications: You love the Lord, and you love children.

During Avalanche Ranch, you'll visit different activities with a group of three to five children. **You're not in charge of preparing or teaching activities; you just get to be there and help children enjoy them as you shepherd your Ranch Crew.**

The following guidelines will help you be the most awesome Ranch Crew Leader.

A Ranch Crew Leader for preschoolers is

- a friend and helper.
- someone who helps children complete activities.
- someone who gets down on the floor to interact with children.
- someone who encourages kids.
- someone who supports Prairie Dog Preschool staff.

During Avalanche Ranch, you'll shepherd a group of up to five preschool children. Your role is to love, encourage, and enjoy the children in your crew. If you've never worked with preschoolers before, the following tips will help you.

- Learn the names of the children in your crew. Call children by name often.

- You'll have 3-, 4-, and 5-year-olds in your Ranch Crew. You'll probably notice big differences in motor skills (such as cutting and coloring) between older and younger children. Help children work at their own pace, and encourage 5-year-olds to help younger children when possible.

- Look into preschoolers' eyes when you speak to them. You may need to kneel or sit on the floor to do this.

- Empower children by offering them choices. Ask, "Would you like to make a craft or play with blocks?" Don't ask, "What do you want to do?" or children may decide they want to do activities that are unavailable or inappropriate.

For Preschool Ranch Crew Leaders Only

As a Ranch Crew Leader for Preschoolers, You'll Be Expected To

- **arrive at least 10 minutes early each day.** Report to the Prairie Dog Preschool area (Day 1) or the Sing & Play Stampede area (Days 2 through 5), and be ready to greet children who arrive early. Your welcoming presence will bring smiles to anxious faces! (Plus, the Prairie Dog Preschool Director may have some special instructions for you.)

- **greet each child by name and with a warm smile.** Help children put on their name badges each day.

- **keep track of your crew members' Prairie Dog Bible Books.** Put these in a Ranch Crew Bag, and keep the bag in a convenient place in your classroom or church at the end of the day.

- **sit with the children in your crew during group activities.**

- **help children choose which Daily Challenge they would like to do.** Talk about how fun it is to help others and share Jesus' love.

- **accompany children to Preschool Craft and Play, Games, and Chadder's Theater.** If necessary, read the instructions at each station, and help children complete the activities. Distribute supplies from the Bible books as needed.

- **repeat the daily Bible Point often.** The more children hear or say the Bible Point, the more likely they are to remember it and apply it to their lives.

- **always check to make sure all children are accounted for before leaving the Prairie Dog Preschool room!** Be sure children hold hands or a rope (called Rodeo Ropes) as you travel. (Never grab, pinch, or pull children as you travel. If a child lags behind, remind him or her to stay with the crew. You may want to walk behind your crew so you can keep all the children in view and avoid traveling too fast.)

- **report any potential discipline problems to the Prairie Dog Preschool Director.** He or she will help you handle problems appropriately.

- **sit with your crew during Showtime Roundup.** Help children participate in each day's show.

- **collect children's name badges and Buddy Bags after each day's Avalanche Ranch.**

- **help children collect their Bible Activity Pages and Daily Challenges, as well as their Bible Point Crafts at the end of each day, so that children can take them home.**

- **release children only to a designated parent or caregiver.** If an unfamiliar adult comes to pick up a child, refer the adult to the Prairie Dog Preschool Director.

- **assist the Prairie Dog Preschool Director with cleanup and preparation for your next meeting.**

THANKS FOR JOINING US AT AVALANCHE RANCH!

Avalanche Ranch Publicity

Here are easy ideas...straight from the horse's mouth!

PROMOTING AVALANCHE RANCH IN YOUR CHURCH AND COMMUNITY

You've planned, prepared, recruited, and trained. You've assembled an awesome team for Avalanche Ranch. Now it's time to promote your program. We've included loads of customizable forms, bulletin inserts, clip art, and much more on the *Clip Art, Song Lyrics, and Decorating* CD. Use your computer expertise, or involve a volunteer computer whiz to help you create dazzling publicity items or jazz up your church's Web site. (*All* Avalanche Ranch clip art is owned by Group Publishing, Inc. You have our permission to use these images to promote Avalanche Ranch for your own church *only*.)

In this section you'll find these additional resources:

- **Invitation to parents**—Fill in your church's information, and then photocopy and mail the parent letter on page 148. If you want to personalize the letter, make any desired changes, and then transfer the letter to your church's letterhead. You can mail the letter to parents in your church or your community.

- **News release**—Adapt the news release on page 149 to fit your church's program. Then submit typed, double-spaced copies to local newspapers, radio stations, and TV stations. A local newspaper may do a story on your church, especially if you do a bang-up job of decorating! Your extra efforts can generate excitement beyond your church walls.

- **Community flier**—Photocopy the flier on page 150, and post copies in local libraries, restaurants, grocery stores, self-service laundries, parks, recreation centers, banks, shopping malls, and schools. Be sure to get permission before posting the fliers. You may also want to check with church members who own businesses in your community. They may be willing to post fliers at their businesses, and they may even suggest additional business owners you can contact.

- **Publicity skit**—Ask for volunteers to perform this publicity skit (p. 151) for your church congregation. The skit will give the congregation a preview of the fun and excitement they can be a part of at Avalanche Ranch.

The following items are also available to help you publicize your VBS. Refer to your Avalanche Ranch catalog for illustrations and prices.

- ***Wah-hoo!* DVD**—You may have already previewed this DVD when you examined your Avalanche Ranch Starter Kit. In addition to being a great leader training resource, the *Wah-hoo!* DVD provides you with a "teaser" to show your congregation. This brief video clip gives church members a sneak peek at Bible Point Crafts, scrumptious Chuck Wagon Chow, and exciting Bible learning that will take place at Avalanche Ranch.

■ **Avalanche Ranch T-shirts**—Invite Avalanche Ranch team members to wear their staff T-shirts to church events in the weeks preceding your program. You may also want to purchase a few iron-on transfers ahead of time and encourage children to wear them on T-shirts at school or in their neighborhoods.

■ *Sing & Play Stampede Music* **audiocassette or CD**—Get kids excited about Avalanche Ranch! Play Avalanche Ranch songs in your Sunday school classes or your other children's ministry programs. (With our volume discounts, you can use these items as an easy fundraiser, too!)

■ **Avalanche Ranch invitation postcards**—Send personalized invitations to all the families in your church and your community. Just fill in the time, date, and location of your Avalanche Ranch program, and drop these postcards in the mail or hand them out at children's ministry events. These colorful postcards are available in packages of 50.

■ **Avalanche Ranch publicity posters**—Hang these attractive posters on church or community bulletin boards to publicize your program. Be sure to include the name and phone number of someone to contact for more information.

If you're hanging a poster in your church, surround it with photographs from last year's program. When parents and kids remember the fun they had last year, they'll be eager to come back for even more Bible-learning fun at Avalanche Ranch.

■ **Giant outdoor theme banner**—Announce Avalanche Ranch to your entire neighborhood by hanging this durable, weatherproof banner outside your church. If parents are looking for summer activities for their kids, they'll know right away that your church has a program to meet their needs.

■ **Avalanche Ranch doorknob danglers**—Hand-deliver information about Avalanche Ranch to families in your community with these bright, lively doorknob danglers.

Choose the items you think will work best in your church and community. Then promote your Avalanche Ranch until you're ready to begin!

Trail Tip Don't overlook the publicity potential in your *Wah-hoo!* DVD (included in your Starter Kit). This DVD includes three short "commercials," designed to help recruit volunteers. Although the emphasis of these commercials is recruitment, you can just as easily use these to get people jumping with excitement about your Avalanche Ranch program.

PUBLICITY

DEAR PARENTS:

Be sure your kids have the greatest summer ever by going to Avalanche Ranch: A Wild Ride Through God's Word! You'll find plenty of adventure at this address:

_____

_____

Each day your children will be a part of fun Bible learning they can see, hear, touch, and even taste! Bible Point Crafts, team-building games, lively Bible songs, and tasty treats are just a few of the Avalanche Ranch activities that help faith grow into real life. Kids will even choose a Daily Challenge—an exciting way to live out what they've learned.

As kids learn about God's love, they'll also enjoy hands-on Bible adventures and daily video visits from Chadder Chipmunk™ (Since everything is hands-on, kids might get a little messy. Be sure to send them in play clothes and safe shoes.) Your kids will even participate in a hands-on missions project called Operation Kid-to-Kid™ that involves nearly a million other children across North America!

Avalanche Ranch is great fun for children of all ages; even teenagers will enjoy signing on as Avalanche Ranch Crew Leaders who help younger children. And parents, grandparents, and friends are invited to join us each day at _____ because that's when we'll be having Showtime Roundup—a daily celebration of God's love you won't want to miss.

So mark these dates on your calendar: _____.

The wild ride starts at _____ and will end at _____.

Call this number _____ to register your children for this

awesome Bible-learning adventure!

Sincerely,

Your Avalanche Ranch Director

PUBLICITY SKIT

Have a few volunteers perform this skit before a worship service, during your announcements, at a midweek program, or during children's church or Sunday school.

SETTING: your church

PROPS: cowboy boots, cowboy hat, chaps (optional), Avalanche Ranch flier, guitar

Harvey steps onstage slowly, giving his best slow, bowlegged amble. He whistles the theme song to "The Good, the Bad, and the Ugly."

Helen: *(Rolls eyes.)* Harvey, what are you doing?

Harvey: *(Tips his hat and speaks in his best, awful John Wayne imitation.)* Just practicin' my amblin', Miss Helen.

Helen: Ambling?

Harvey: Would you prefer that I mosey? *(Changes his walk slightly to another over-the-top cowboy walk.)*

Helen: I'd prefer that you take off that silly get-up and get ready to head home. We're going to be late and the Martins are coming over for lunch—

(Harvey takes out a guitar and begins singing off-key)

Harvey: *(Singing)* Oh give me a home where the buffalo roam, where the deer and the antelope play.

Helen: Harvey!

(Harvey continues to sing.)

Helen: *(Louder)* Harvey!

(Harvey continues to sing.)

Helen: *(Yelling)* Harvey!

(Harvey drops his guitar in surprise.)

Helen: Does this have *anything* to do with the announcement in today's bulletin about Avalanche Ranch?

Harvey: *(Excitedly)* It's a wild ride through God's Word—wah-hoo!

Helen: Well, you're welcome to volunteer…*(takes guitar)* but probably *not* to lead singing. And it doesn't start until [your VBS dates], so you can take off those ridiculous clothes until then! Now, let's go home and have lunch with the Martins and you can think a little bit more about what you'd like to do at Avalanche Ranch.

Harvey: Maybe I should leave these on and get one of those mechanical bulls. Then I'd *really* be ready!

(Helen sighs and walks off with Harvey's guitar.)

Have your pastor or Avalanche Ranch Director come up to give the details of the times and dates of your Avalanche Ranch and how to register or sign up to volunteer.

Registration

Follow these instructions, and you'll soar through registration!

MAKING AN UNFORGETTABLE IMPRESSION

Start generating excitement and enthusiasm for Avalanche Ranch before the adventure begins!

The excitement starts with preregistration. About a month before your scheduled Avalanche Ranch, begin preregistering children in your church. With your new Web Toybox, preregistration is a snap: Just send people to your Avalanche Ranch Web site and have them fill out a registration form. When they click "Submit," kids will instantly be assigned to a crew!

If you're not planning to use your Web Toybox, just make copies of the "Avalanche Ranch Registration Form" (p. 172), and have parents fill them out. Save the completed registration forms; you'll use them to assign Ranch Crews (described on page 156).

To pique kids' (and parents') interest in preregistration, try incorporating some of the following activities:

- **Show the *Wah-hoo!* DVD overview clip in your church worship service and Sunday school sessions.** This video clip gives everyone in your church a chance to preview Avalanche Ranch and see what an impact Group's VBS can have.

- **Have Sunday school classes work together to turn their rooms into Avalanche Ranch settings.** Provide rolls of bulletin board paper (available at most school- and teacher-supply stores). Let kids cut out ranch animals such as horses or cows.

- **Chart your preregistration in eye-catching ways.** Decorate a wall or bulletin board with some thematic décor. Each time someone preregisters, add another decoration. Here are some variations you can try:

  - Create a herd of crazy, colorful cows. Each time someone preregisters, add a wacky cow to the herd.

  - Set out your Avalanche Ranch display, and add a paper horseshoe to the ranch entrance every time a child registers.

  - Cover a bulletin board with brightly colored bandannas. When children preregister, add a small pair of paper boots.

When it's time for Avalanche Ranch to begin, you'll have a wonderful wall decoration to show that kids are stampeding to your VBS.

The excitement continues as kids arrive at Avalanche Ranch. At registration, remember that some families from your community are coming into contact with your church for the first time. You don't want their first impression to be of long, boring registration lines. To make an unforgettable impression, try the following ideas:

"Registra-tion is always so hard! How can I make it easier?" Our best tip to you: Follow these instructions *exactly* as they're written. We've heard from VBS directors from across North America who were skeptical. But when they followed these simple step-by-step instructions, it worked! Remember, we've made the mistakes during our field tests—so you don't have to!

Clever VBS directors have told numerous success stories of letting middle schoolers and high schoolers work on decorations. One director had a group of fifth- and sixth-graders work on decorations during a lock-in the week before VBS began. Aside from setting a spectacular stage for VBS, it was a great way to involve older kids and help them be an important part of the program.

REGISTRATION

- **Set up the Avalanche Ranch display behind your registration table.** This welcoming ranch entrance will help kids feel like they're walking into a real dude ranch! You can even set up imitation Christmas trees or pine-scented cardboard trees (available from Group Publishing or your local Group distributor) near the entryway.

- **Play the *Sing & Play Stampede Music* CD.** The fun, upbeat music will provide a festive atmosphere.

- **Distribute sample Chuck Wagon Chow grub.** You can use a snack from the Chuck Wagon Chow Leader Manual, or you can come up with your own. Be sure to include drinks, especially if the weather's hot.

GET READY FOR AN AVALANCHE OF FUN!

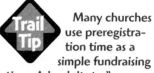

Many churches use preregistration time as a simple fundraising time. Ask adults to "sponsor" one or more children who will attend VBS. (Post the total number of children you're expecting at VBS so people have an idea of the number of kids you need to sponsor.) The sponsorship fee can be monetary or a food donation for Chuck Wagon Chow. We've heard of churches funding their entire VBS program through these easy donations!

EXTRA IDEA!

If you want to start your VBS with a big bang, consider planning an all-church Avalanche Ranch kick-off. Decorate your fellowship hall, church lawn, or a nearby park, and set up one or more of the following "stations."

- Have a Pony Express Relay. Stuff a pillow case with crumpled paper "letters," and have participants carry three bags of letters from one end of the playing area to the other.

- Set out a rubber horseshoes set, and have players try their hand at this classic game.

- Bring in a rocking horse, and let players take turns "roping" the horse with a jump rope.

- Serve up steaming cowboy chili, and provide the ingredients for root-beer floats (don't forget the frosty mugs!).

- Set cowboy hats about 10 feet from a rope line. See who can pitch the most pennies into a cowboy hat.

Be sure to have at least one person videotaping your party. You can use the edited footage for further promotion—this year or in years to come!

SETTING UP RANCH CREWS

Trail Tip

Prayerfully consider the responsibility of setting up Ranch Crews. These small groups have a powerful impact on children, helping them form special relationships and memories.

Field Test Findings

A few years ago, the registrar at a field test church placed pre-K children into elementary crews. These little ones struggled to clearly understand the lessons, which are designed for older children. We quickly moved most of them into Prairie Dog Preschool, where they had a much more meaningful, memorable, age-appropriate experience.

Trail Tip

We've heard from directors who place all 5-year-olds in one group of Ranch Crews and have them rotate together through the elementary program. This may seem like a nifty way to include pre-kindergartners, but be aware that the elementary program is designed and tested for children who have completed kindergarten. Plus, these little ones will miss out on the wonderful relationship-building opportunities of being in a mixed-age group in Prairie Dog Preschool. Don't rob kids of this awesome experience!

REGISTRATION

One week before Avalanche Ranch begins, assign preregistered kids to Ranch Crews. (Remember, if you're using your Web Toybox, this will be done automatically as kids register. All you'll do is add a crew leader and you're ready to go!)

Participating in Ranch Crews is an important part of kids' Avalanche Ranch experience, so use care and consideration when making Ranch Crew assignments. Follow the guidelines given in the planning section of this manual under "One Week Before Your Avalanche Ranch" (p. 66). If you don't know very many of the kids who will attend Avalanche Ranch, ask Sunday school teachers or other Christian education workers to help you assign kids to crews.

STEP 1: INVENTORY YOUR REGISTRATIONS

■ **When you're ready to assign crews, make nine copies of the "Age-Level Roster" form (p. 168).** Label the forms with grades K, 1, 2, 3, 4, and 5; do the same using "3-year-olds," "4-year-olds," and "5-year-olds" (for 5-year-olds who have not yet attended kindergarten). List the names of preregistered kids on the appropriate age-level rosters.

■ **Count how many kids have preregistered for your Avalanche Ranch, and divide them into two groups: elementary-age children and preschool-age children.** Elementary-age children have completed kindergarten, fifth grade, or any grade in between. Be sure to check forms carefully; some families may have registered more than one child on one form. If children who have completed sixth grade want to participate in your program, that's OK; keep in mind, though, that most of the Avalanche Ranch activities are designed for slightly younger kids. Avalanche Ranch is designed to use young people in grades six and higher in leadership roles, so encourage mature sixth-graders to serve as Assistant Ranch Crew Leaders. For other ideas about how upper-elementary kids can participate in Avalanche Ranch, see page 34.

STEP 2: DETERMINE HOW MANY RANCH CREWS YOU'LL HAVE

■ **Each Ranch Crew will have no more than five kids and one adult or teenage Ranch Crew Leader.** (Preschool crews may have a high school leader.) Divide the total number of preregistered elementary-age kids by five to discover how many elementary Ranch Crews you'll have. Do the same with preschool preregistrations. Use the line below to help you determine this.

If you want to encourage kids to bring their friends to Avalanche Ranch, you may want to place only three or four kids in each crew. This will allow you to add to your crews. (We've found that it's a good idea not to fill all of the crews, since most crews *will* grow.)

Once you've determined the number of preschool and elementary crews you'll need, check to see that you've recruited enough Ranch Crew Leaders. Remember that you'll need a Ranch Crew Leader for every crew, plus a few extra leaders on hand on Day 1.

Number of (elementary or preschool) kids _____ / at five kids per crew = Number of Ranch Crews_____.

MAKE IT EASY!

Once you've determined the number of Ranch Crews you'll have, ask volunteers or Avalanche Ranch staff to help create a complete Ranch Crew Bag for each Ranch Crew. Place the following items inside each Crew Bag:

- ■ permanent marker
- ■ 5 name badges
- ■ 5 lengths of string (1-yard long)
- ■ 5 Wild Ride Bible Guides or Prairie Dog Bible Books
- ■ 5 Avalanche Ranch sticker sheets

You may want to staple a list of the crew members' names to the bags so they can see who will be in their crews. On Day 1, simply give Ranch Crew Leaders their bags, and they'll be ready for the fun to begin!

REGISTRATION

For guaranteed success, follow this registration plan exactly!

■ **Photocopy the "Ranch Crew Roster" form (p. 169).** You'll need one form for every four Ranch Crews.

■ **Assign a Ranch Crew Leader to each Ranch Crew.** It's helpful to indicate whether the leader is an adult (A), a teenager (T), or a junior higher (J).

■ **Set up preschool Ranch Crews.**
Gather the age-level rosters for ages 3, 4, and 5. Beginning with the 3-year-old age-level roster, assign one child from each preschool age-level roster to each preschool Ranch Crew. Since each crew has five spaces, you'll have more than one representative of some age levels in each crew. Remember, it's helpful to have a mixture of preschool ages in each crew so that crew leaders can work with 3-year-olds, while 5-year-olds may be a bit more self-sufficient. Be sure to check off the names on the age-level rosters as you assign them to crews.

■ **Set up elementary Ranch Crews.**
Gather the elementary age-level rosters. Beginning with the kindergarten age-level roster, assign one child from each age-level roster to each Ranch Crew. Since each crew has only five spaces, you won't be able to have every age level in every crew. Check off the names on the age-level rosters as you assign them to crews. Refer to the following examples for ways to spread age levels evenly among your Ranch Crews.

You aren't *required* to group children in combined-age Ranch Crews, but we strongly recommend it because it works so well. Children, whether younger or older, help one another throughout their time together. Plus, you'll minimize discipline problems because the diversity frees children from the need to compete with peers of the same age. For more information on the benefits of combining ages, see page 32.

If you have an equal number of children in each grade level,

- fill one-third of your crews with kids who have completed kindergarten and grades two through five.

- fill one-third of your crews with kids who have completed grades one through five.

- fill one-third of your crews with kids who have completed kindergarten through grade four.

If you have an abundance of younger children,

- group kindergartners, second-graders, third-graders, and fifth-graders together. Assign two kindergartners to each crew if necessary. Remind Ranch Crew Leaders to encourage

REGISTRATION

Field Test Findings Our Ranch Crew Leaders are always amazed at how well kids work together in a multi-age setting! Most kids truly enjoy being with children of other ages, and your discipline problems will practically disappear. However, if some children insist on being with same-age friends, put pairs of friends in the same Ranch Crew or in the same lettered group. This allows children to be with their buddies, while giving them wonderful opportunities to interact with kids of other ages and abilities.

the fifth-graders to help younger children. Fifth-graders might even be named Assistant Ranch Crew Leaders.

- group kids in grades one through four together. Assign two first-graders to each crew if necessary.

If you have an abundance of older children,

- group kindergartners, first-graders, second-graders, and fourth-graders together. Assign two fourth graders to each crew if necessary.

- group grades two through five together. Assign two fifth-graders to each crew if necessary.

If you have fewer than five kids per Ranch Crew,

- vary the age-level mix, if possible, so you'll have open spaces in your program at every age level. These spaces can be filled by kids who haven't preregistered.

STEP 4: COMPLETE THE MASTER LIST

■ **Double-check to make sure you've assigned each participant to a Ranch Crew.** Then write kids' Ranch Crew numbers on their registration forms next to their names.

■ **Alphabetize the registration forms, and then transfer kids' names and crew numbers to the "Alphabetical Master List" (p. 171).** Put a P in the crew-number space next to each preschooler's name.

■ **Give the preschool registration forms, age-level rosters, and Ranch Crew rosters to the Prairie Dog Preschool Director.**

Bring the "Age-Level Roster" lists, "Ranch Crew Roster" lists, and "Alphabetical Master List" with you to registration!

Trail Tip

It's a good idea to keep gender in mind when assigning children to Ranch Crews. If at all possible, be sure to include more than one child of each gender. Even though Avalanche Ranch activities are designed to help kids work together, kids will feel at ease more quickly if there are a few members of their own gender in the group.

REGISTRATION

LET RANCH CREW LEADERS HELP WITH SIGN-IN

Ranch Crew Leaders can help you breeze through registration. They meet and greet kids and help keep kids busy while others are standing in line. Read on to find out how Ranch Crew Leaders help make registration a snap.

RANCH CREW LEADER REGISTRATION SUPPLIES

Each Ranch Crew Leader will need the following supplies:

- permanent marker
- colorful washable markers or posters
- 1 sheet of poster board
- 1 Ranch Crew Bag
- copy of the "Ranch Crew Roster" for his or her crew
- masking tape

Each child will need a Wild Ride Bible Guide and a name badge strung on 1 yard of yarn or string. Give these items to the Ranch Crew Leaders, and have them store the items in their Ranch Crew Bags.

RANCH CREW LEADER REGISTRATION PROCEDURES

- Give each Ranch Crew Leader a cowboy hat to wear. This helps station leaders and kids recognize crew leaders.

- When Ranch Crew Leaders arrive, they'll write their Ranch Crew numbers on sheets of poster board and then hang the crew-number posters *where they can be seen easily* in the Sing & Play Stampede area. It helps if leaders hang the posters in numerical order.

- After children complete the registration process, they'll meet their Ranch Crew Leaders by their crew-number posters in Sing & Play Stampede.

- Ranch Crew Leaders will greet kids and welcome them to Avalanche Ranch. Leaders will use permanent markers to write kids' names and crew numbers on their name badges. If additional kids have been assigned to Ranch Crews during registration, Ranch Crew Leaders will update their copies of the "Ranch Crew Roster."

- Ranch Crews will work on decorating their crew-number posters while they wait for others to arrive. This is a fun time for Ranch Crew Leaders and crew members to get acquainted.

Be sure to post the crew posters numerically so kids can easily find their crew leaders on the first day. Through the week, rotate the crew posters each day so new kids can sit near the front and really tune in to the program. It's a super way to keep everyone in on the action!

Having Ranch Crew Leaders write kids' names on their name badges is a nice way for leaders to learn the names of their crew members. Plus, they can make them all large and legible.

REGISTRATION DAY IS HERE!

REGISTRATION SUPPLIES

For registration, you'll need the following supplies:

- entry decorations such as hay bales, saddles, Bible Point posters, and inflatable ranch animals

- 3 tables

- 4 signs:

  ✔ "Preregistered—completed kindergarten through fifth grade"

  ✔ "Walk-in registration—completed kindergarten through fifth grade"

  ✔ 2 "Preschool registration" signs with arrows pointing to Prairie Dog Preschool

- 2 copies of each completed elementary "Ranch Crew Roster" (p. 169)

- 1 copy of each completed preschool "Ranch Crew Roster" (p. 170)

- 3 copies of each completed elementary "Age-Level Roster" (p. 168)

- 2 copies of each completed preschool "Age-Level Roster" (p. 168)

- 2 copies of the completed "Alphabetical Master List" (p. 171)

- plenty of pens and pencils

- at least 5 volunteers, including the registrar

- chairs for your volunteers

- blank copies of the "Avalanche Ranch Registration Form" (p. 172)

REGISTRATION SETUP

Before registration, set up two tables in your church's foyer or entry area. If weather permits, you may want to set up your tables outside to allow more room. (It's a good idea to place these tables far apart to avoid a bottleneck.) Put the "Preregistered—completed kindergarten through fifth grade" sign above one table. Put the "Walk-in registration—completed kindergarten through fifth grade" sign above the other table. Set up chairs for your volunteers at each table. Be sure to place your signs high enough for everyone to clearly see them.

Field Test Findings

One field test host church did an amazing job of preparing for registration. Registration helpers were visible everywhere, with clipboards containing all the information for preregistered kids. Parents could breeze in, find out where their children went, and get everyone "delivered" easily. This extra-mile preparation spoke volumes to the parents—many of whom expected chaos on that first day of VBS. (Needless to say, they were pleasantly surprised!) Remember, parents are hesitant to drop off their children if everything looks chaotic. More than ever, they'll expect a safe environment in which to place their children.

Trail Tip

If you used your Web Toybox, simply print out the completed crew rosters and place them at the preregistered table. Then follow the instructions on these pages to get any walk-ins registered. After Day 1, simply log in to your Web Toybox and update the crew rosters.

Trail Tip

You may want to give each Ranch Crew Leader a few extra name badges and 1-yard lengths of string for walk-in registrants who may join their crews.

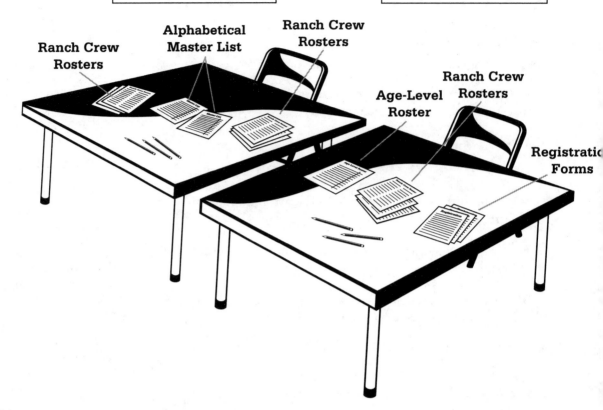

Preregistered
K–5th Grade

Walk-In
Registration K–5

Ranch Crew
Rosters

Alphabetical
Master List

Ranch Crew
Rosters

Age-Level
Roster

Ranch Crew
Rosters

Registration
Forms

Trail Tip

It's helpful to tape lists and rosters to the registration tables. That way they won't blow away or get lost or torn. Plus, registration helpers will have easy access to all information and can easily scan the lists to find a child's name. It also removes the temptation for one person to pick up and carry away the vital information.

PREREGISTERED TABLE

On the table below the preregistered sign, place

- 1 copy of the completed "Alphabetical Master List" (p. 171),
- 1 copy of each completed "Ranch Crew Roster" (p. 169), and
- several pencils.

WALK-IN REGISTRATION TABLE

On the table below the walk-in registration sign, place

- 1 copy of each completed elementary "Age-Level Roster" (p. 168),
- 1 copy of each completed "Ranch Crew Roster" (p. 169),
- copies of the "Registration Form" (p. 172), and
- several pens or pencils.

TAKE THE EXPRESS LANE!

Consider an "Express Preregistered Check-In" system. Have a couple of volunteers stand at the entryway, holding copies of the "Alphabetical Master List." Kids who are preregistered can tell the "express checkers" their names and have the checkers look at the list to see which Ranch Crews kids are in. Or if you're low on volunteers, enlarge your "Alphabetical Master List," and post several copies of it near your registration area. Kids (and parents) can check the list to find which Ranch Crews they're in and then simply find their crew numbers and Ranch Crew Leaders.

PRESCHOOL REGISTRATION TABLE

Set up a table (or several if you have more than 25 preschoolers) outside your Prairie Dog Preschool area. Put the two "Preschool registration" signs (with arrows pointing to Prairie Dog Preschool) near your main registration area.

On the preschool registration table(s), place

- 1 copy of each completed preschool "Age-Level Roster" (p. 168),

- 1 copy of each preschool "Ranch Crew Roster" (p. 170),

- blank copies of the "Registration Form" (p. 172), and

- several pencils.

REGISTRATION: HERE THEY COME!

1. Arrange for your registration workers (including Ranch Crew Leaders) to arrive at least 30 minutes before registration is scheduled to begin.

2. Cut apart the individual "Ranch Crew Roster" lists from the third set of "Ranch Crew Roster" lists you copied. As Ranch Crew Leaders arrive, give each a copy of his or her crew roster.

3. Send elementary Ranch Crew Leaders to the Sing & Play Stampede area and preschool Ranch Crew Leaders to Prairie Dog Preschool. Explain that as kids arrive, they'll find their Ranch Crew numbers at the registration tables and then join their crew leaders and other Ranch Crew members in Sing & Play Stampede or Prairie Dog Preschool.

4. Assign two workers to the preregistration table, two workers to the walk-in table, and at least one worker to the preschool table.

5. Go over the registration instructions for each area (preregistered, walk-in registration, and preschool). Answer any questions workers have, and offer the following helpful hints:

- Kindly insist that each participant fill out a complete registration form, including all pertinent health and emergency information. *This is very important!*

- If families have both preschool and elementary children, encourage them to go to the preschool area first. This will keep preschoolers from getting fidgety as they wait for their parents to register their older siblings.

- Walk-in registration will naturally take more time. As families are filling out their registration forms, scan the Ranch Crew rosters for openings. This will help you complete Ranch Crew assignments quickly.

After you've answered all the questions, have registration workers and Ranch Crew Leaders take their places. You're ready to welcome kids to Avalanche Ranch!

Trail Tip

It's important that you have a completed registration form for *each child*, not just one for each family! When families place all their children on one form, it can be difficult to find information that's specific to each child.

Field Test Findings

We discovered that it was *parents* (not so much the children) who had the biggest objection to mixed-age groups. Our director patiently explained the benefits of combined-age learning over and over and over. To save your time (and sanity), it's a good idea to have copies of the parent letters (pp. 173-174) on hand to help explain why you've set up your program in this nontraditional, yet beneficial, way.

IMPORTANT! It's important that you know at all times who is in each Ranch Crew. In an emergency or if a parent needs to pick up a child midprogram, you'll want an accurate "map" of where everyone is.

AFTER REGISTRATION

After registration on Day 1, shout out a loud, "Wah-hoo!" Your biggest job is done! Read on to find out how you can ensure that Days 2 through 5 are successful.

- **Leave your registration tables in place.** You'll want to continue welcoming children as they arrive on Days 2 through 5, as well as registering any newcomers. Tape the "Alphabetical Master List" to the table, and set out several pencils or pens. To chart attendance, let children (or parents) check each day's box as they come to Avalanche Ranch. (Or set out a laptop computer and use the Attendance Tracker feature on your Web Toybox.)

- **Update your online information.** Add any walk-in registrations to your online database. This will allow you to have information for *all* families at your fingertips!

- **Check in with Avalanche Ranch Station Leaders and Ranch Crew Leaders.** Even if you've taken care of the details ahead of time, unforeseen glitches can mar your adventure. After you've gone through one day's activities, meet with your staff to evaluate how things went. Station leaders may find that they need additional supplies or alternative room assignments. Inexperienced Ranch Crew Leaders may be having trouble handling unruly children in their Ranch Crews. If this is the case, you may need to reassign some children to different crews or rearrange your groups so Ranch Crews with inexperienced leaders visit stations with crews that have experienced leaders.

- **Update your "Alphabetical Master List" and "Ranch Crew Rosters" as needed.** Be sure to check with the volunteers at the walk-in table. Kids who completed walk-in registration on Day 1 can be added to the "Alphabetical Master List" for speedier check-in through the rest of the week. If you've rearranged your Ranch Crews, make sure each Ranch Crew receives an updated "Ranch Crew Roster."

REGISTRATION

YOU DID IT! NOW SIT BACK AND ENJOY THE ADVENTURE!

AVALANCHE RANCH REGISTRATION INSTRUCTIONS

Photocopy these instructions, and place copies in all registration areas. Have registration workers highlight their areas of responsibility.

PRESCHOOL: PREREGISTERED AND WALK-IN

Preschool registration will take place _____.

1. Greet family members or caregivers with a warm smile. Thank them for bringing their children to Avalanche Ranch.

2. Ask for each child's name and age (3, 4, or 5 years old). Greet each child by name, and thank him or her for coming.

If a child has completed kindergarten or is older than 6, send the family to the elementary preregistered line.

3. Have parents or caregivers complete registration forms for unregistered children.

4. Locate each registered child's name on the "Alphabetical Master List," and place a check mark on the Day 1 box to indicate that he or she is present.

5. If a child is a walk-in, scan the preschool "Ranch Crew Roster" lists to find an appropriate Ranch Crew to place him or her in. Add the child's name to the "Alphabetical Master List" as well.

6. Point out the child's Ranch Crew Leader, and have a Prairie Dog Preschool volunteer guide the child to the Ranch Crew Leader.

7. Tell the family members or caregivers where they can pick up their preschoolers each day. Assure them that an adult or teenage Ranch Crew Leader will stay with children until the family members or caregivers arrive.

ELEMENTARY: PREREGISTERED

Elementary registration will take place _____.

1. Greet family members or caregivers with a warm smile. Thank them for bringing their children to Avalanche Ranch.

2. Ask for each child's name and the grade he or she last completed (kindergarten through fifth grade). Greet each child by name, and thank him or her for coming.

If a child has not yet attended kindergarten, send the family to Prairie Dog Preschool for registration.

3. Locate each child's name on the "Alphabetical Master List," or if a child's name isn't on the list, send the family to the walk-in table to complete a new registration form.

4. Put a check mark by each child's name to indicate that he or she is present at Avalanche Ranch. Then tell the child his or her Ranch Crew number and crew leader's name.

5. Direct children to the Sing & Play Stampede area, and explain that crew leaders are waiting there with name badges. Tell children to look for the large signs with their crew numbers on them.

6. Tell the family members or caregivers what time they can pick up their children each day. Encourage them to come early and participate in Showtime Roundup.

ELEMENTARY: WALK-IN REGISTRATION

Elementary registration will take place _____.

1. Greet family members or caregivers with a warm smile. Thank them for bringing their children to Avalanche Ranch.

2. Ask for each child's name and the grade he or she last completed (kindergarten through fifth grade). Greet each child by name, and thank him or her for coming.

If a child has not yet attended kindergarten, send the family to Prairie Dog Preschool for registration.

3. Add each child's name to the appropriate "Age-Level Roster." Have the child's parent or caregiver complete a registration form.

4. While parents fill out registration forms, assign each child to a Ranch Crew. Check the box for allergies or other needs. Refer to the "Ranch Crew Rosters" to see which crews have openings. Look for a Ranch Crew *without* a member in that child's grade. *If you have questions about assigning children to Ranch Crews, see your director!*

5. Write each child's Ranch Crew number on his or her completed registration form. (Later you'll need to add the new name and Ranch Crew assignment to the "Alphabetical Master List.")

6. Direct children to the Sing & Play Stampede area, and explain that crew leaders are waiting there with name badges. Tell children to look for the large signs with their crew numbers on them.

7. Tell the family members or caregivers what time they can pick up their children each day. Encourage them to come early and participate in Showtime Roundup.

AGE-LEVEL ROSTER

GRADE: _____

Name   Name

_____   _____
_____   _____
_____   _____
_____   _____
_____   _____
_____   _____
_____   _____
_____   _____
_____   _____
_____   _____
_____   _____
_____   _____
_____   _____
_____   _____
_____   _____
_____   _____
_____   _____
_____   _____

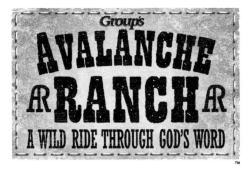

RANCH CREW ROSTER

Ranch Crew Number: _____

Ranch Crew Leader: _____

Assistant Crew Leader: _____

RANCH CREW MEMBERS

ALLERGY

1._____ ❑
2._____ ❑
3._____ ❑
4._____ ❑
5._____ ❑

Ranch Crew Number: _____

Ranch Crew Leader: _____

Assistant Crew Leader: _____

RANCH CREW MEMBERS

ALLERGY

1._____ ❑
2._____ ❑
3._____ ❑
4._____ ❑
5._____ ❑

Ranch Crew Number: _____

Ranch Crew Leader: _____

Assistant Crew Leader: _____

RANCH CREW MEMBERS

ALLERGY

1._____ ❑
2._____ ❑
3._____ ❑
4._____ ❑
5._____ ❑

Ranch Crew Number: _____

Ranch Crew Leader: _____

Assistant Crew Leader: _____

RANCH CREW MEMBERS

ALLERGY

1._____ ❑
2._____ ❑
3._____ ❑
4._____ ❑
5._____ ❑

Ranch Crew Roster

Ranch Crew Number: _____

Ranch Crew Leader: _____

Assistant Crew Leader: _____

Ranch Crew Members

ALLERGY

1. _____ ❑
2. _____ ❑
3. _____ ❑
4. _____ ❑
5. _____ ❑

Ranch Crew Number: _____

Ranch Crew Leader: _____

Assistant Crew Leader: _____

Ranch Crew Members

ALLERGY

1. _____ ❑
2. _____ ❑
3. _____ ❑
4. _____ ❑
5. _____ ❑

Ranch Crew Number: _____

Ranch Crew Leader: _____

Assistant Crew Leader: _____

Ranch Crew Members

ALLERGY

1. _____ ❑
2. _____ ❑
3. _____ ❑
4. _____ ❑
5. _____ ❑

Ranch Crew Number: _____

Ranch Crew Leader: _____

Assistant Crew Leader: _____

Ranch Crew Members

ALLERGY

1. _____ ❑
2. _____ ❑
3. _____ ❑
4. _____ ❑
5. _____ ❑

DEAR PARENTS:

We're so glad you've signed up your child for an exciting week on Avalanche Ranch. This VBS program will give your child a wild ride through God's Word.

You'll notice that things at Avalanche Ranch are...well, a little different from what you might be used to. For one thing, elementary kids will be in mixed-age groups with other children who have finished kindergarten through grade 5. These small groups, called Ranch Crews, are led by adults or teenagers who love children and love the Lord. Ranch Crews are an important part of Avalanche Ranch! But you still might have some doubts...

My child won't come if he can't be with his friends. While it's true that your child might not get to be with his or her very best friend, your child *will* have wonderful opportunities to make new friends and interact with a new group of children. Most of us assume that age-graded classes are the best way to go, simply because that has been our only experience. However, studies indicate that children choose to play with children of other ages. Studies show that children learn as much—or more—when they're linked with kids of different ages. In fact, one study observed that children naturally chose to play with other children their age only 6 percent of the time. They played with children who were at least one year older or younger than they were 55 percent of the time. Encourage your child to try something different—he or she might be surprised!

My child won't like being with little kids. Parents are continually surprised that, after a few days of VBS, their older children *love* this newfound role! Suddenly, they're the "cool" big kids with younger children looking up to them. And while your child is helping younger kids with simple tasks like reading and writing, he or she is having the chance to serve and demonstrate Christ's love! It's a meaningful way to discover—and practice—the joy of service.

My child will get trampled by those bigger kids. Avalanche Ranch is carefully designed for groups of multi-age children. That means games are noncompetitive, team-building activities (brilliantly disguised as wildly fun games) in which your child's abilities will shine. In fact, many games are designed to *highlight* the importance of smaller kids. It's more likely that your younger child will be loved, affirmed, and doted upon by his or her older crew mates.

You'll have to water down the Bible lessons so everyone can learn. Since Avalanche Ranch doesn't rely on more traditional teaching methods (like fill-in-the-blank puzzles or word searches), kids *experience* Bible stories in powerful, life-changing ways. And that's something kids of *all* ages will enjoy...and remember. Then crew leaders gather with kids for small-group discussion. These are questions that apply to every child but may touch each child at a different level. For example, on Day 3 as we learn that God is strong, a crew leader might ask, "When do you depend on God's strength?" A younger child might respond, "During a scary storm," while an older child with more experience with life's challenges may say, "When my friends are all doing something I know is wrong."

Millions of children have experienced this multi-age approach with Group's VBS, with surprise and delight at the outcome. Children's ministry experts agree that combining ages has numerous benefits: teaching children to work together, experiencing what it means to be a family, and serving others in love. However, the most important factor in making this program a success is your attitude. If your child has doubts, reassure him or her that this is a wonderful opportunity to try something new. Your support will speak volumes to the children we're serving.

We look forward to ministering to your child at Avalanche Ranch.

Avalanche Ranch Director

Dear Parents:

We're so glad you've signed your child up for an exciting week at Avalanche Ranch. This VBS program will give your little one a wild ride through God's Word.

You'll notice that things at Avalanche Ranch are...well, a little different from what you might be used to. For one thing, preschoolers will be in mixed-age groups with other young children, ages 3- through 5-years-old. These small groups, called Ranch Crews, are led by adults or teenagers who love children and love the Lord. Ranch Crews are an important part of Avalanche Ranch! But you still might have some doubts...

My 5-year-old will be bored with all these little kids. Five-year-olds play an important role in their Ranch Crews. Pre-kindergartners now become the "big kids" who can cut with more accuracy, glue more easily, and (gasp) even write their names! Younger children will *love* being with your child and will show their affection generously. All this admiration is wonderful for your child's self-esteem and allows him or her to serve younger children in hands-on, practical ways.

My 3-year-old will get hurt by those older kids. Actually, younger children will be loved, served, and doted on by their older crew mates. Plus, in a mixed-age small group, a crew leader has much more time to spend one-on-one with your child. And you can be sure that Avalanche Ranch activities are all specially designed just for mixed-age groups, so younger children won't be in over their heads.

My child won't come if she can't be with her friend. While it's true that your child may not be able to be with her very best friend, she will have the opportunity to make many new friends. Studies show that children learn as much—or more—when they're linked with kids of different ages. In fact, one study observed that children naturally chose to play with other children their age only 6 percent of the time. They played with children who were at least one year older or younger than they were 55 percent of the time. If your child really needs the security of a familiar face, we can most likely pair him or her with one special friend.

Millions of children have experienced this multi-age approach with Group's VBS, with surprise and delight at the outcome. Children's ministry experts agree that combining ages has numerous benefits: teaching children to work together, experiencing what it means to be a family, and serving others in love. However, the most important factor in making this program a success is your attitude. If your child has doubts, reassure him or her that this is a wonderful opportunity to try something new. Your support will speak volumes to the children we're serving.

We look forward to ministering to your child at Avalanche Ranch.

Prairie Dog Preschool Director

Trail Tips

Here are great tips from our herd to yours!

DAILY STAFF DEVOTIONS

Plan to meet with your station leaders and Ranch Crew Leaders for 15 to 20 minutes before your program begins each day. Use this time to give announcements, address questions or concerns, and pray together. Ministering to children is rewarding but hard work, so you may also want to refresh your staff daily with an encouraging devotional. The following devotions tie into the daily Bible Points and help your staff understand the importance of these Points in the lives of children.

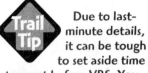

Due to last-minute details, it can be tough to set aside time to meet before VBS. You may want to use these devotions after each day's program as a reflection and encouragement to your staff. (You may need to provide child care in order for some of your staff to attend.)

DAY 1

BIBLE POINT: GOD IS REAL.

SUPPLIES: CD player, *Sing & Play Stampede Music* CD, butcher paper, marker, tape, Wrangler Ringer

Before everyone arrives, hang the sheet of butcher paper in the front of the room. Welcome your staff, and thank them for serving at your Avalanche Ranch VBS.

Say: **I'm so glad that each one of you is here today to help teach kids that GOD IS REAL. Let's take a minute to think about how that relates to each of our daily lives. Kids are going to be learning about how the people of Jericho were afraid of the Israelites. In fact, Rahab told the Israelites that the people's hearts were melting in fear! Wow!**

Find one or two friends sitting near, and take 30 seconds each to tell one another what your greatest fear is. It could be heights, illness, retirement, or even spiders! Allow staff members to forms groups. Then say: **Are you ready? Go!**

While groups are sharing, play "The Great Adventure" from the *Sing & Play Stampede Music* CD. After several minutes, sound the Wrangler Ringer to get everyone's attention.

Say: **OK, let's hear what some of your greatest fears are.** Encourage people to call out some fears, and write them in a column on the left-hand side of the butcher paper hanging at the front of the room. Then ask:

■ **What do some of these fears have in common?** (They're out of our control; they're bigger than us.)

■ If we remember that **GOD IS REAL,** how does it change how we handle our fears? (It puts them in perspective; they don't seem so big.)

Say: **Next to each fear, let's write something we know about God that will help put that fear in perspective. For example, if the fear is losing your job, we could write, "God will provide for us."** Allow people to call out ideas to write next to each fear.

Then say: **Our verse for today is "The Lord is the only true God"** (Jeremiah 10:10). **Because GOD IS REAL, all these things we wrote down are true! Let's pray now to commit this day to God, remembering that he is real!**

Pray: **Dear God, thank you for allowing each of us here today to touch the lives of children. Help us remember in each moment of our days that you are real, and help us minister to these children today with your love. In Jesus' name, amen.**

DAY 2

BIBLE POINT: GOD IS WITH US.

SUPPLIES: CD player, *Sing & Play Stampede Music* CD, Wrangler Ringer

Welcome your staff, and say: **Today kids are going to learn that GOD IS WITH US. Our Bible story is about how God was with the Israelites when they crossed the Jordan River, as they prepared to enter the Promised Land. They were on the verge of something great, but they still had to pass through something challenging to get there. The river was rushing at flood stage, maybe 10 to 12 feet high, and I bet a lot of the Israelites were skeptical about getting across. But God was there, and he provided a way.**

Right now, take a few moments to think of a hard time or challenging situation you've experienced. Then think of an item you have with you right now that can represent that tough situation. For example, your car keys could represent a car accident you've experienced or a scar could represent an illness or surgery you've had. Be creative!

Allow staff a few moments to think. Then say: **Now get in groups of two or three and tell one another about the item you've chosen and what it represents.** Play "God Is Good (All the Time)" from the *Sing & Play Stampede Music* CD while groups are discussing. After groups have had a chance to discuss, sound the Wrangler Ringer to get their attention. Then ask groups to answer the following questions together, pausing after each question. Ask:

■ **When you were going through this particular time, did you realize that God was with you? Explain.**

■ **What's a practical way you can remember today (and from now on!) that God is with you?**

When groups have had time to discuss, say: **Our verse today says, "For the Lord your God is with you wherever you go" (Joshua 1:9). Isn't that incredible? No matter where we are, God is there, desiring that we turn to him and his strength. Let's pray and commit our day to God.**

Pray: **Dear God, thank you so much that you're with us wherever we go. Thank you that you love us and you want to be our strength in every situation. Help us serve and love these children as we help them understand that you are with us. In Jesus' name, amen.**

DAY 3

BIBLE POINT: GOD IS STRONG.

SUPPLIES: CD player, *Sing & Play Stampede Music* CD, Wrangler Ringer, 16-ounce bottles of soda or water (be sure the bottles are new, with the caps still sealed), cups and ice (optional)

As staff members enter, give each person a bottle of soda or water. (If the beverage isn't chilled, provide cups of ice as well.) Direct staff members *not* to open their drinks yet.

Say: **I've brought each of you a nice, cool, refreshing beverage to thank you for all of your hard work at Avalanche Ranch. Here's the catch. Only** [name of a staff member] **can use both hands to open the bottle. The rest of you can use only one finger. Go ahead and enjoy your drinks!**

Play "Worship You Forever" from the *Sing & Play Stampede Music* CD while participants try to open their drinks. Most will opt to hand the bottle to your selected volunteer to have him or her open the bottle. When the song ends, or when everyone is enjoying a drink, ask:

■ **Why did you give your bottles to** [name of volunteer]?

■ **How is that like the way we rely on God's strength?**

Say: **When times are tough, we turn to God because GOD IS STRONG. Just like the children's song says, "We are weak, but he is strong."**

Find a partner, and discuss one area in your life where you need to rely on God's strength. Then pray for your partner, asking God to provide that person with the strength he or she needs.

Quietly play "You Are My All in All" from the *Sing & Play Stampede Music* CD in the background. When all pairs have finished praying, close by saying, **In Jesus' name, amen.**

DAY 4

BIBLE POINT: GOD IS AWESOME.

SUPPLIES: CD player, *Sing & Play Stampede Music* CD, Wrangler Ringer, paper, pen and pencils, butcher paper, marker, tape

Before staff members arrive, hang the butcher paper at the front of the room. Welcome your staff, and thank them for all their hard work at Avalanche Ranch.

Say: **Our Bible Point and story for today are really exciting. Kids are going to learn about how Jesus died and rose again and that GOD IS AWESOME! We hear the word** *awesome* **a lot, and sometimes we don't even think about what it really means. Let's think about that. Find a couple of friends sitting nearby.**

Allow time for staff to find partners, and give each group paper and a pen or pencil.

Continue: **Now take a few minutes with your group to brainstorm what the word** *awesome* **means. Write the phrases you come up with on your sheet of paper. You'll have one minute.** While groups are brainstorming, play "Awesome God" from the *Sing & Play Stampede Music* CD. After one minute, sound the Wrangler Ringer to get everyone's attention.

Say: **Let's share what you came up with. Each time someone writes a definition of** *awesome* **on our sheet of paper, I'd like another group to tell how it applies to God. For example, if your definition is "something that evokes wonder," someone might say, "It fills us with wonder that Christ died and rose again."** Let volunteers come forward to write what they shared, and encourage others to tell how that applies to God.

Just looking at this sheet, it's clear that GOD IS AWESOME! Let's praise God for [read some of the things written on the paper]!

Form a circle and join hands. Say: **I'll start the prayer, and the person to my right will continue by praying one of the examples we have written on the butcher paper. When we run out of examples, you can think of your own or end the prayer by saying, "In Jesus' name, amen."**

Pray: **Dear God, you are so awesome! Thank you that you died and rose for us...**

Trail Tip

On Day 4 children will hear the message of Jesus' death and resurrection. Since this may be a natural time for children to ask questions about salvation, you may want to photocopy and distribute the "Helping Children Follow Jesus" section (p. 181) to each staff member. Or refer leaders to the Crew Leader Pocket Guide.

TRAIL TIPS

DAY 5

BIBLE POINT: GOD IS IN CHARGE.

SUPPLIES: Wrangler Ringer

Welcome staff, and thank and congratulate them on helping kids learn about God.

Say: **Today's our last day together, and we're going to help teach kids that GOD IS IN CHARGE. Because God is in charge, we need to obey his commandments. Let's see what that's like.**

Form partners. Continue: **Now each person think of something out of the ordinary or downright silly to command your partner to do. (Make sure it's not something that could endanger anyone, though!) For example, you could command your partner to hop up and down on one foot while singing the national anthem.** Give people 15 seconds to think. **OK, now take turns commanding your partners and following their commands.** After a minute or two, use the Wrangler Ringer to get everyone's attention.

Ask:

■ **How did it feel to have to do what** *someone else* **wanted you to do?**

■ **Did it seem like there was any real reason to follow their commands?**

■ **How is this like or unlike obeying God?**

Say: **Hopefully we can relate a little more to how kids might feel when they're asked to obey. Of course God doesn't ask us to do anything for no reason—he's good and knows what is best. We can trust that God's ways are right, so it's good that GOD IS IN CHARGE.**

Pray: **God, we praise you that you're real, you're with us, you're awesome, and you're strong. We love you, and we want to obey your commandments. Help us be good examples to these children today of what it means to obey you. In Jesus' name, amen.**

TRAIL TIPS

Trail Tip
This is a good time to distribute any thank you gifts or notes you've brought for your staff, such as the Howdy plush toy.

HELPING CHILDREN FOLLOW JESUS

At Avalanche Ranch, children don't just hear about Jesus' love; they see it, touch it, sing it, taste it, and put it into action through Daily Challenges. As they travel from station to station, they go deeper into their understanding of God. Most important, children learn that God sent his Son, Jesus, to die for our sins because he loves us.

You'll notice that there's no "set" time for children to make a faith commitment. We feel that Avalanche Ranch helps children build relationships—with other children, with adults, and with Jesus. And since each child is at a different point in his or her relationship with Jesus, programming a time for commitment may be confusing to some children. However, if it's part of your church tradition to include a time for children to make a faith decision, feel free to add it in during Showtime Roundup on Day 4.

Some children may want to know more about making Jesus part of their lives. If you sense that a child might like to know more about what it means to follow Jesus as a forever friend, give this simple explanation:

God loves us so much that he sent his Son, Jesus, to die on the cross for us. Jesus died and rose again so we could be forgiven for all the wrong things we do. Jesus wants to be our forever friend. If we ask him to, he'll take away the wrong things we've done and fill our lives with his love. As our forever friend, Jesus will always be with us and will help us make the right choices. And if we believe in Jesus, someday we'll live with him forever in heaven.

You may want to lead the child in a simple prayer inviting Jesus to be his or her forever friend. You may also want to share one or more of the following Scripture passages with the child. Encourage the child to read the Scripture passages with you from his or her own Bible.

- John 3:16
- Romans 5:8-11
- Romans 6:23
- Ephesians 2:4-8

Be sure to share the news of the child's spiritual development with his or her parent(s).

Build Wild Faith at Home

Take Home
These Great Items!

EQUIP FAMILIES WITH EXCITING RESOURCES

WHY ARE FAMILY RESOURCES SO IMPORTANT?

Your Avalanche Ranch will reach a variety of children from countless backgrounds. Each of these children (and their families) can benefit from having Avalanche Ranch resources at home. The following family resources not only remind kids of Avalanche Ranch fun but also provide excellent Bible reinforcement for months after your program has ended. A *Sing & Play Stampede Music* audiocassette may be the only Christian music heard in some children's homes.

WHAT ARE FAMILY RESOURCES?

We hear from families and children's workers every year who say their kids love items such as the *Sing & Play Stampede Music* CD and *Chadder's Wild West Adventure* video or DVD. In fact, although we provide more media products each year, we keep selling out of them and have to order more!

Kids love to have mementos of their time at Avalanche Ranch. Avalanche Ranch T-shirts, caps, and iron-on transfers make great reminders of your program. (And remember, all items are returnable, so there's no risk!)

HOW CAN FAMILIES GET THESE RESOURCES?

We realize you're busy; after all, you're directing a VBS program! So we've made it simple to get these important items into the hands of the kids in your program.

Make it extra easy for families to take home VBS fun by setting up a store that's filled with reminders of Avalanche Ranch. Stock your store with items such as *Sing & Play Stampede Music* audiocassettes, CDs, and videos or DVDs; Chadder videos or DVDs; Avalanche Ranch water bottles; Howdy plush toys; T-shirts; and iron-on transfers. Then set a price for each item. Decide how much money you'll earn on each item you sell. Remember, any money you make can go to your church's missions or children's ministry program or to local community outreach programs.

Then set up shop! Place the items on a table just outside the Showtime Roundup area. Post your prices clearly where everyone can see them. Staff your store with a few willing volunteers (or youth group members), and "open your doors" after Showtime Roundup ends. You'll be amazed at the stampede!

TRAIL TIPS

RECOMMENDED ADVANCE ORDER QUANTITIES

Item	Quantity
Chadder's Wild West Adventure video or DVD 	10 percent of VBS enrollment
Sing & Play Stampede Music audiocassette or CD	75 percent of VBS enrollment
Sing & Play Stampede Music video or DVD 	10 percent of VBS enrollment
Howdy plush toy	20 percent of Prairie Dog Preschool enrollment
Avalanche Ranch water bottle	10 percent of VBS enrollment
Avalanche Ranch Mailable Foto Frame	75 percent of VBS enrollment

IT'S THAT EASY!

HEALTH AND SAFETY CONCERNS

Each station leader manual gives safety tips for specific station activities. As director, however, you're responsible for larger health and safety concerns that may affect the entire VBS. The information below may alert you to health and safety concerns that require your attention.

HEALTH ISSUES

You'll want to maintain a first-aid kit in a central station. Stock your first-aid kit with adhesive bandages of different sizes, first-aid cream, antibacterial ointment, sterile gauze pads, and insect repellent. You may also want to provide a place for children to lie down if they feel ill. Keep children's registration forms near your first-aid area so that you can call parents or caregivers in case of serious injury.

Your Avalanche Ranch registration form provides a place for parents or caregivers to identify food allergies. Dairy allergies are common, but you may also have children who are allergic to gluten (wheat, rye, barley, or oats), nuts, or other foods.

Most of the snacks suggested in the Chuck Wagon Chow Leader Manual will require only slight modifications for children with food allergies. Consult with the Chuck Wagon Chow Leader about modifying snacks or substituting flavored rice cakes, popcorn, fruits, or raw vegetables to accommodate children with food allergies.

INSURANCE: MAKE SURE YOU'RE COVERED

Your church probably already has an insurance policy or policies that are intended to protect you from loss as a result of fire, theft, injury, or lawsuits. Your program is probably covered by your regular insurance, but you should double-check with your insurance agent to be sure. You're not likely to have serious injuries, but you'll want to be prepared just in case.

FACILITIES: KEEPING THE ROUNDUP SAFE

Many accidents can be prevented by well-maintained facilities. After you've selected station meeting areas, check each area for potential hazards. Remove broken or dangerous items, and be sure to lock storage areas that contain chemicals, cleaning solutions, or other toxic materials.

Your church is about to become a high-traffic area! Keep in mind that you'll probably need to clean bathrooms and empty trash daily. You'll also want to spot-check hallways, lobbies, and meeting rooms for trash, stray Ranch Crew Bags, and lost-and-found items.

TRAIL TIPS

CHILD ABUSE: KEEPING KIDS SAFE

Child abuse can take many forms. While you may feel sure that no one in your church would physically or sexually abuse a child in your program, emotional abuse or neglect can be harder to detect. Prevent child abuse by enlisting only staff members that you know and trust and by discussing your concerns and expectations with them ahead of time.

Avalanche Ranch field test directors reported few or no discipline problems. But you'll want to talk with your staff about how you'll handle any that do arise. Discuss appropriate and inappropriate staff responses to situations that require discipline. Photocopy and distribute the "What's a Ranch Crew Leader?" handout from pages 139 and 143 of this manual. This handout suggests positive-language responses for easy classroom management. Remind staff members that you expect them to model God's love in all they say and do.

Avalanche Ranch activities are designed so that children are always supervised by a station leader and several Ranch Crew Leaders. You may want to point this out to parents who are concerned about adequate supervision. To avoid even the appearance of impropriety, encourage each staff member to avoid spending time alone with a child. Suggest that staff members escort children in pairs or small groups for bathroom and drinking fountain stops. A good rule for safe touching is to never touch a child where his or her bathing suit would cover.

Use these health and safety tips to set up an Avalanche Ranch program that ensures the physical, emotional, and spiritual well-being of everyone involved.

Trail Tip Some churches require volunteers to go through a short class, seminar, or workshop on appropriate actions when working with children. This is an excellent idea, especially if less-experienced teenagers and adults will be helping out. Check with your church leaders to see if they know of (or have led) a class that would be helpful to you. Or check out www.childrensministry.com. There you'll find back issues of Children's Ministry Magazine containing articles on making your church a safe place.

Trail Tip The Crew Leader Pocket Guide (one for elementary leaders and one for preschool leaders) is filled with practical, easy tips on child safety. Be sure to equip your staff with these handy guidebooks!

TRAIL TIPS

KIDS WITH SPECIAL NEEDS

PHYSICAL DISABILITIES

If you know you'll have physically challenged children at your program, you'll need to make sure your station areas are wheelchair accessible. You may also want to recruit a staff member to look out for these children. This staff member can ask parents or caretakers about specific needs such as

- whether kids have special equipment such as wheelchairs,
- what kids can and cannot eat,
- what kids need help doing,
- what kids like to do for themselves, and
- what kids enjoy most.

Because children work together and help one another in Ranch Crews, most physically challenged children will get the help they need from their crew members and Ranch Crew Leaders. However, if a physically challenged child needs constant help to participate in station activities, consider assigning an additional Ranch Crew Leader to his or her crew. For this position, choose someone who will be sensitive and who is capable of responding to the child's needs. You might even suggest reading a current resource on special needs ministry, such as *Special Needs—Special Ministry* (Group Publishing, Inc.).

Physically challenged children may be shy, but often they're very bright and innovative. Ranch Crew Leaders can encourage them to shine in stations that include group discussion, such as Chadder's Wild West Theater or Wild Bible Adventures. (Plus, as kids carry out their crew roles, they'll all discover how important each crew member is!)

LEARNING DISABILITIES

Educators estimate that up to 20 percent of today's children have some type of learning disability. This means that in a program of 100 children, up to 20 kids could be battling with dyslexia, attention-deficit/hyperactivity disorder, or other learning disabilities. Kids with learning disabilities aren't lazy or dumb—they just learn differently from other children.

Avalanche Ranch works for children with learning disabilities! Here's why:

- **It doesn't rely heavily on reading skills.** Children who enjoy reading can volunteer to be Readers for their Ranch Crews. Children who have trouble reading can choose other, equally important jobs.

- **It allows kids processing time.** Because each Ranch Crew has a Ranch Crew Leader, station leaders don't have to single out kids who need special help. Crew leaders can help the kids in their

Ranch Crews work at their own pace. And station leaders are free to go around and check in with children as they complete their activities.

■ **It doesn't require children to think sequentially.** Fifty percent of all students are frustrated by sequential-type assignments. At Avalanche Ranch, children don't have to master a new set of information each day. Instead, they learn one basic Point that's reinforced in different ways for different kinds of learners.

If you know or suspect that kids with learning disabilities will be attending your program, let your leaders know. Encourage them to help these children by

■ giving instructions one at a time,

■ using the positive-language suggestions in the "What's a Ranch Crew Leader?" handout (pp. 139 and 143) or the Crew Leader Pocket Guide,

■ ignoring harmless annoying behaviors, and

■ praising children sincerely and often.

For more information on attention-deficit/hyperactivity disorder (ADHD), use the address below to contact Children and Adults With Attention-Deficit/Hyperactivity Disorders.

Children and Adults With Attention-Deficit/Hyperactivity Disorders
8181 Professional Place, Suite 150
Landover, MD 20785
www.chadd.org

Field Test Findings

We've received many touching letters and e-mail messages from parents of special-needs children. These adults were surprised and delighted at how much their kids got out of Group's VBS. Parents of special-needs kids are used to classroom situations and children's ministry functions that are unwelcoming and difficult for their kids. It's a delight to hear that this VBS model is friendly and effective for all types of children!

TRAIL TIPS

Avalanche Ranch Follow-Up

The wild fun can continue long after Avalanche Ranch!

THANKS FOR JOINING US AT GROUP'S AVALANCHE RANCH!

Admit it—as much fun as it was to go to Avalanche Ranch, it's a great feeling to be finished. And why not? After all, you just succeeded in putting on a top-notch, high-quality, Bible-based, and downright fun program for a group of wiggly kids! Such effective ministry takes a lot of mental, emotional, and physical energy. So now you can sit back and thank God for blessing your program. Then congratulate yourself and your staff on an awesome adventure! In this section, you'll find ideas that will help you wrap up your program and follow up with children and their families. You'll also find helpful evaluation forms you can use to get specific feedback from station leaders and Ranch Crew Leaders.

CLOSING PROGRAM: WILD BIBLE FUN

Reach out to parents, grandparents, and friends *every day* at Avalanche Ranch!

If you want an easy way to give parents and church members a glimpse of Avalanche Ranch fun, invite them to attend Showtime Roundup. This fun-filled Bible-learning time is already built into your Avalanche Ranch program each day. Explain that parents can join the fun by arriving just 20 minutes early when they come to pick up their children. They'll see children singing Sing & Play Stampede songs, telling what they did in each station, and actively reviewing the daily Bible story. Parents will really catch the Avalanche Ranch spirit as children celebrate God's love with a grand celebration on Day 5.

If you want to have a separate closing program, follow the steps below to set up a station "open house." Set up your open house in the evening or even on Sunday morning. Parents and kids will love it!

1. **Have station leaders set up the following activities in their respective station areas.** If you purchased additional *Sing & Play Stampede Music* CDs and audiocassettes, encourage station leaders to play the Avalanche Ranch songs while people are visiting their areas.

Have the Sing & Play Stampede Leader teach words and motions to all 10 songs (or as many as time allows). Or let kids request their favorites!

FOLLOW-UP

Have the Prairie Dog Preschool Director set up five or six Prairie Dog Preschool activities that children can visit with their parents. Choose from the activities suggested below, or let the preschool director suggest kids' favorites.

- Wade in the Water
- Build 'Em Up, Knock 'Em Down
- Up, Up, and Away
- Doctor Spot

 Have the Cowpoke Crafts and Missions Leader display the sample Bible Point Crafts (or have kids display the crafts they made—if they're willing to part with them for a little while). Let adults make Buddy Bags or Make-Your-Own Sheriff's Badges.

 Have the Horseplay Games Leader lead families in the One and Only game from Day 1 or the Empty the Pail game kids played on Day 3.

 Have the Chuck Wagon Chow Leader set out supplies for making Stick With You S'Mores. Display a sample snack, and let children and parents make their own tasty treats.

Have the Chadder's Wild West Theater Leader play the *Chadder's Wild West Adventure* video.

 Have the Wild Bible Adventures Leader set up the Jordan River from Day 2. Families can experience standing near the "rushing river" and then gather stones to make their own memorials.

 Have the Showtime Roundup Leader lead people in the show from Day 5, and then show off the mountain of warm, cuddly Prayer Bears that kids made for orphans in Africa.

2. **Begin by having everyone gather in the sanctuary or the fellowship hall for a brief introduction and a Sing & Play Stampede time.** Have your Sing & Play Stampede Leader teach everyone the theme song, "Wild Ride!" This is a great time to distribute Avalanche Ranch completion certificates.

3. **Designate a 30- to 45-minute time frame in which families can visit the stations.** At the end of the designated time, use a Wrangler Ringer to call everyone back to your original meeting area for Showtime Roundup. Let parents share what it was like to see kids living out the Daily Challenge. (You'll capture some amazing stories!)

4. **Thank everyone for coming, and encourage them to join you in planning and preparing for next year's program.**

FOLLOW-UP IDEAS

Your Avalanche Ranch has ended, but helping kids know and love Jesus never ends. You still have lots of time to share the good news about Jesus with the kids in your church and community. The outreach efforts you make will help you share God's love with your Avalanche Ranch participants and their families. Use the ideas below to design a follow-up plan that fits your church's needs.

- **Send Avalanche Ranch follow-up postcards.** Kids love getting mail, so here's a surefire way to get kids back for Sunday school—a personal invitation from Avalanche Ranch. These colorful postcards help you make a long-term impact on kids by involving them in your regular Sunday school program. (Order these postcards from Group Publishing or your Group supplier.)

- **Give away Avalanche Ranch photos.** Deliver framed photos to families of children who don't regularly attend your church. Kids will treasure these colorful, fun mementos, and you'll have an opportunity to invite the family to visit your church. (Order Avalanche Ranch Mailable Foto Frames from Group Publishing or your Group supplier.)

- **Invite Chadder Chipmunk to visit a children's ministry event.** Schedule a return engagement of *Chadder's Wild West Adventure* during another children's ministry event. Children who visited your church during Avalanche Ranch will want to come back and revisit their furry friend. You might even have a volunteer dress in the Chadder costume. Kids will love a visit from a giant, huggable Chadder! (Order *Chadder's Wild West Adventure* DVD and Chadder costume patterns from Group Publishing or your Group supplier.)

- **Bring back Rowdy.** Each day at Sing & Play Stampede, you have the option of doing a skit featuring a goofy cowboy named Rowdy. Kids and parents will love seeing Rowdy again in "Rowdy's Return," a 30-minute closing production. Rowdy returns along with some of his friends to learn more at Avalanche Ranch. Simply visit www.group.com/vbs to download your complete script and setup instructions.

- **Sponsor a parents' day.** Build relationships with children's parents by having a parents' day during Avalanche Ranch. Encourage children to invite their parents or older siblings to join them. Provide adult and youth Bible studies, or have family members visit the stations with their children's Ranch Crews. Also require parents to come inside to pick up their children so you can make contact with them.

Field Test Findings

We heard that a church held a Chadder Movie Night where kids watched the Chadder movie in its entirety. Kids loved the video so much that the children's director even pulled out Chadder videos from past years! The event was such a hit that they've planned another one.

■ **Hold an Avalanche Ranch memory night.** Invite all the Avalanche Ranch participants to a get-together every month or every quarter. Make each memory night a fun event that fits the Avalanche Ranch theme. Serve Chuck Wagon Chow, play Sing & Play Stampede tunes, and play Horseplay Games. Show slides or video footage of your adventure. You may even interview kids about what they're doing now that the adventure has ended.

■ **Thank your staff members for all their hard work.** Your praise and appreciation will speak volumes to your volunteers and can be integral in their decision to volunteer next year. So go the extra mile to show them how much you appreciate all they've done. A card with a personal, heartfelt message is always a good idea. Balloons, flowers, Howdy plush toys, or baked goodies are even better. Volunteers will appreciate a gift certificate to a local ice cream shop, along with a note that reads, "It was cool having you at Avalanche Ranch!" Or present each helper with a tin camping mug filled with flavored coffee beans and a note saying, "You sure perked things up at Avalanche Ranch." Look for more fun thank you gifts at www.groupoutlet.com.

■ **Sign up a team for next year's program.** It's never too early to start recruiting, and your staff will be excited about the week they've just finished at Avalanche Ranch. There's no better time to collect the names of volunteers who might be interested in volunteering for next year's VBS program. Photocopy the "Join the Team!" handout on page 194, and post it around your facility. You may be surprised at the jump-start you'll get on next year's recruitment!

Be among the first to find out what Group's 2008 VBS theme is by going to www.group.com/vbs/2008 on July 9, 2007!

FOLLOW-UP

JOIN THE TEAM!

As part of our team, you made Avalanche Ranch a great time! We would love to have you join our team for another adventure at next year's VBS. If you're interested, just sign below. We'll hang on to your name and information and let you know about opportunities for next year.

NAME	PHONE	AT NEXT YEAR'S VBS, I WOULD BE INTERESTED IN...

EVALUATING YOUR AVALANCHE RANCH PROGRAM

After Avalanche Ranch you'll want to check in with your station leaders, Ranch Crew Leaders, and other staff members to see how things went.

Photocopy the "Ranch Station Leader VBS Evaluation" (p. 196) and the "Ranch Crew Leader VBS Evaluation" (p. 197), and distribute the photocopies to your staff. To help your evaluation process go smoothly, you may want to ask staff members to return their evaluations within two weeks of Avalanche Ranch. After two weeks, specific details will still be fresh in staff members' minds, and they'll have a good perspective on their overall experiences.

After you've collected Ranch Station Leader and Ranch Crew Leader evaluation forms, please take a few moments to fill out the "Avalanche Ranch Evaluation" online at www.group.com/vbs. Be sure to summarize the comments you received from station leaders and crew leaders. Your detailed feedback will help us meet your needs as we plan an all-new program for next year.

Thanks for being so wild about God!

FOLLOW-UP

RANCH STATION LEADER VBS EVALUATION

Thanks for joining us at Avalanche Ranch!
Please complete this evaluation form to help us plan for next year's VBS.

1. I led the _____ Station.

2. Were the instructions in your station leader manual clear and easy to follow? Explain.

3. What did you like best about your station? What did kids like best?

4. What would you like to change about your station?

We want every Group resource to help you create a learning experience that will "Wow" your kids. How are we doing?

	UH-OH				WOW!
■ Kids enjoyed the learning experiences…they were fun!	1	2	3	4	5
■ Kids were excited to come back to this station.	1	2	3	4	5
■ The materials were easy for me to prepare and teach.	1	2	3	4	5
■ The activities helped kids connect to the Bible story and/or Bible Point.	1	2	3	4	5
■ The activities worked the way they were supposed to.	1	2	3	4	5
■ Kids remembered the Bible Points.	1	2	3	4	5
■ The materials (crafts, student books, music) were appealing to kids.	1	2	3	4	5

RANCH CREW LEADER VBS EVALUATION

Thanks for joining us at Avalanche Ranch!
Please complete this evaluation form to help us plan for next year's VBS.

1. What was the best thing about working with your Ranch Crew?

2. What was the hardest thing?

3. Did the "For Ranch Crew Leaders Only" handouts or Crew Leader Pocket Guide help you as you worked with kids? Explain.

4. What's one thing you would like more help with in your role?

We want every Group resource to help you create a learning experience that will "Wow" your kids. How are we doing?

	UH-OH				WOW!
■ Kids enjoyed the learning experiences—they were fun!	1	2	3	4	5
■ Kids were excited to come back to Avalanche Ranch.	1	2	3	4	5
■ The activities helped kids connect to the Bible story and/or Bible Point.	1	2	3	4	5
■ The activities worked the way they were supposed to.	1	2	3	4	5
■ Kids remembered the Bible Points.	1	2	3	4	5
■ The crafts were appealing to kids.	1	2	3	4	5
■ Kids liked the Chadder video.	1	2	3	4	5
■ Kids enjoyed the Sing & Play Stampede music.	1	2	3	4	5
■ The student books were engaging and fun for kids.	1	2	3	4	5
■ The experiences were memorable and unique—for the kids *and* adults!	1	2	3	4	5
■ We saw evidence of life application through the Daily Challenges.	1	2	3	4	5
■ I got positive feedback from parents.	1	2	3	4	5
■ I saw kids form friendships with their crew leaders and crew members.	1	2	3	4	5

INDEX